GOD

IS A

VERB!

Selah!
Stop &Think Intently

LYNN KELLER

GOD IS A VERB!
SELAH! STOP &THINK INTENTLY

iUniverse books may be ordered through booksellers or by contacting:

iUniverse
1663 Liberty Drive
Bloomington, IN 47403
www.iuniverse.com
844-349-9409

ISBN: 978-1-6632-1594-9 (sc)
ISBN: 978-1-6632-1596-3 (hc)
ISBN: 978-1-6632-1595-6 (e)

Library of Congress Control Number: 2021919162

Print information available on the last page.

iUniverse rev. date: 09/28/2021

CONTENTS

ORIENTATION

This book began in my first class at Cornell University. We were asked whether the purpose of religion was to believe in Jesus or to be nice to others. I was the sole student who chose the Golden Rule. The results likely would be different these many years later, but at the time, it was shocking to me, as not everyone was even a Christian. Even then, there should have been a debate. Did others think this was a right-or-wrong question? Was this about getting a good grade, rather than getting an education?

Later in the lecture, our instructor said that at Cornell, we would learn *how* to think, rather than *what* to think.

That class not only set the tone for me at Cornell but for the rest of my life as well, particularly about God and religion and philosophy.

Bucky Fuller, the American author, systems theorist, and futurist, said it best for me: "Faith is much better than belief. Belief is when someone else does the thinking."

In these decades, I have found it particularly bizarre to have been told what I think or believe; often, as a rule, it is about what they believe, not what I believe or think or care.

This book is my journey since that day at Cornell, continuing with values and concepts always at my core. I always pay attention to the patterns, so perhaps my journey will support yours. I consider the two trees to be an organizing system, not a belief system.

When I was four, I could not remember which came first, six or seven, because they both began with an *s*. I told my father that I should only be expected to count one number past my birthday.

My father said, "Ross is only two, and he can count to ten. I am thirty-two, and I can count past one hundred."

Just then, I looked over his shoulder and saw the clock! Aha! I had a cheat sheet. Numbers had a place and an order. Tens went in a line and twelves went in a circle. Numbers had relationships and patterns. There were sets. Numbers mattered in their sets.

To this day, I always consider whether a person is counting numbers or identifying a set; most importantly, whether it is by tens or twelves. How does eleven matter? What about thirteen?

Later that day, I surprised my mother to no end. I was doing well with math, so she asked, "What is six times eight?"

Almost instantly, I responded, "Forty-eight." My life changed that fast. I no long was limited by counting. I changed dimensions.

A late friend once identified himself as a "compassionate atheist." He lived this "way of return" without ever getting waylaid in beliefs. Would you discuss your faith with him?

My first class at Cornell was called "Orientation." What is important? Is it how you think or what you believe? Did God exist before thinking?

The core distinction is whether God is a noun or a verb.

That is the foundation for this book.

THE PROBLEMATIC MODEL

> In order to change an existing paradigm you do not struggle to try and change the problematic model. You create a new model and make the old one obsolete. That, in essence, is the higher service To which we are all being called.
>
> —Buckminster Fuller

God, as a *noun*, is the problematic model. "God who?" is the problem. The new model is "God is a verb." The paradigm will shift.

Our soul is a verb in the image of God.

God is a Verb: Selah takes Bucky's advice very seriously.

It made sense to add the word *selah*. Selah is found seventy-one times in Psalms. It means "stop and think." It is an imperative in this book. Do not just slide over a thought, particularly if you have just heard it for the first time.

This book takes on the challenge of the existing concepts since God created Adam and Eve in the garden of Eden. All the people on this planet earth have been in this paradigm for 5,781 years. The paradigm that "God is a verb" directly challenges the interpretation of the entire story of Adam and Eve. We accept what happened. It is the total lack of comprehension we change radically. This is a paradigm shift that will require considering our context and our entire history.

Every story has to be rethought. Does Aquarian Age thinking begin with clarity about God? *God Is a Verb* discusses how to think about God, not what to believe about God. Selah.

Our paradigm shifts, first of all, in realizing that God is not a noun. God is not a person, an *it*, or a thing. He is not corporal and has no boundaries.

"In the beginning, God created …" The very first thing God did was create. God is the act of creating. It is by actions that God is known. God was not something that was created. God was the process, the creating.

We instantly get past definitions and opinions that are nouns. God is the loving, the knowing, the perceiving. Our ideas flow and reverberate. All the rules and definitions that fit precepts of God as a noun are instantly obsolete. We can begin to have a discussion based on feelings and inner sense. We can share our experiences and emotions. God, as a big king in the sky, becomes absurd. God is no longer a judge, a ruler, a decider. Literally, God is love. Love is a verb.

I SEE GOD

by Buckminster Fuller

I see God in
the instruments and the mechanisms that
work
reliably,
more reliably than the limited sensory departments of
the human mechanism.
And God says
observe the paradox
of man's creative potentials
and his destructive tactics.
He could have his new world
through sufficient love
for "all's fair"
in love as well as in war
which means you can
junk as much rubbish,
skip as many stupid agreements
by love,
spontaneous unselfishness radiant.

The revolution has come—
set on fire from the top.
Let it burn swiftly.
Neither the branches, trunk, nor roots will be endangered.
Only last year's leaves and
the parasite-bearded moss and orchids
will not be there
when the next spring brings fresh growth
and freestanding flowers.

Here is God's purpose—
for God, to me, it seems
is a verb
not a noun,
proper or improper;
is the articulation
not the art, objective or subjective;
is loving,
not the abstraction "love" commanded or entreated;
is knowledge dynamic,
not legislative code,
not proclamation law.
not academic dogma, not ecclesiastic canon.
Yes, God is a verb,
the most active,
connoting the vast harmonic
reordering of the universe
from unleashed chaos of energy.
And there is born unheralded
a great natural peace,
not out of exclusive
pseudo-static security
bit out of including, refining, dynamic balancing.
Naught is lost.
Only the false and nonexistent are dispelled.

And I've thought through to tomorrow
which is also today.
The telephone rings
and you say to me
Hello Buckling this is Christopher; or
Daddy it's Allegra; or
Mr. Fuller this is the Telephone Company Business Office;
and I say you are inaccurate.
Because I knew you were going to call
and furthermore I recognize
that it is God who is "speaking." And you say
aren't you being fantastic?
And knowing you I say no.

All organized religions of the past
were inherently developed
as beliefs and credits
in "second hand" information.

Therefore it will be an entirely new era
when man finds himself confronted
with direct experience
with an obviously *a priori*
intellectually anticipatory competency
that has interordered
all that he is discovering.

(Reprinted from *Whole Earth Catalog*, Fall 1968)

I was a subscriber to the *Whole Earth Catalog* from its beginning. It was a fountain of new ideas. Upon reading the above poem, the most important words to me were, "Yes, God is a verb, the most active, connoting the vast harmonic reordering of the universe."

These words became my paradigm for God.

"Including, refining, dynamic balancing" became the process, the action, the verbs.

Concept

A rose has a front
A rose has a back
God has neither a front nor a back
God does not have corporeality
He has no body
He has no limits
Roses have substance
God does not
Rather than thinking about God as a form with the characteristics
and qualities of physical presence, we shift to actions, movement, and
attributes of happening and being

GOD IS A VERB

When asked to describe Himself, God said, "Yud He Vauv He." This is regularly translated as, "I Am that I Am." More properly, the translation is "I shall be as I shall be." What a difference a verb makes! The tense of the verb is all-telling and all-meaning. Present tense is an *is*. It is a reality. It is current and established. The tense does not indicate anything other than a presence in the present tense.

The future tense creates a paradigm shift for the concept of God. By God stating Himself in a future tense, He creates a different reality. God is a changing reality. God becomes *doing* rather than an *it*. God is action, not form. Considering God as a verb requires thinking about every single aspect concerning God in a new context.

"I shall be as I shall be" indicates a future tense. God is changing and becoming as the process of creating. Past and present tenses would mean a God already formed, a noun.

Hebrew is read from right to left. Notice there is an opening on the far left in the left side of the letter *He* or *Het*. This means that people can choose to leave, but there is always the opening to return.

Rather than thinking about God as a form, with the characteristics and quality of physical presence, we shift to actions and attributes of happening and being. We begin thinking about wind and light and temperature and time. We suddenly look at God as the Creator as a manifesting entity or action, rather than as a big magician in the sky. Imagine the force that creates the tiniest triangle as a neutron, to complexities of physical beings, to our solar system and the cosmos. The concept of the force is akin to the creation as a state of being.

God as an action is creation.

> Moses said to G-d: "Behold, when I come to the Bnei Yisrael ... and they will say to me ... What is His Name?' what shall I say to them." G-d said to Moses: "I shall be as I shall be" has sent me to you.'" (Exodus 3:13–14)

We take the same words and shift parts of speech. God, a noun, becomes God, a verb, an action.

God Is a Verb including the poems are not Kabbalah, a Jewish mystical system. There are no secrets, no mysteries. It is a change in definition. However, there are some metaphysical concepts that are valid for this book, as both are concerned with our relationship with God and with the two trees in the garden of Eden.

Beyond the tree is the *Ein Sof,* which are aspects of God that are beyond our capacity to comprehend. Ein Sof means "without end." Nouns, as a concept, generally have form and limits. One of the seventy-two names of God is *Bal Tachlis,* which means God is not bound or limited in any way. As a verb, God is the action in the heavens, rather than a being, a noun, in the sky. God does not have a beginning or an end, both of which would be considered boundaries. Any form of the physical would be bounded. God is not bounded by time or place.

Furthermore, the challenge for us is to discover God's relationship to us as human beings on planet earth, rather than to attempt to understand God, other than in a variety of aspects. He is totally beyond human. Thus, we concentrate on attributes of God that are comprehensible.

The very concept of God as a verb shifts the focus into relationship, rather than form and limitations of boundaries.

The attributes of God shift in language. Adjectives, which apply to God, do not apply to verbs. Words describing God and God's characteristics do not apply to rules of grammar. God is compassionate, but compassion is a noun. Compassion, however, implies doing. That is a limitation of language, not of God.

The problem is that nomenclature that relates to human concepts and labels—as to verbs, adverbs, adjectives, and nouns—skews the communication. We are left with terminology to describe the inexplicable, with terms that limit and alter the intention. The words used herein are aimed at the context of the statement, "A rose is a noun. God is a verb." Attributes are used as defining actions and characteristics of God, who is an action, a state of being and awareness without physicality. The inadequacies of our languages are indications of our inability to conceive of God as a consciousness.

We are taught that God has many dimensions, of which we can only identify and approximate a few. Some dimensions and characteristics are comprehensible in the abstract but not achievable. Certainly, most aspects of God are far beyond our human experience and comprehension.

The challenge for us is to bring all our comprehension, actions, and reactions into the most basic levels. The more clarity we have in the most elementary concepts, the more aligned we can be to our purpose for being and our life on this planet.

Since God is not a noun, consider this truth: God does not have a form in any criteria. Since God is not a noun, God cannot and does not have a gender. Most animals have gender and come in pairs. God creates pairs but is never other than One. The pronouns *he*, *she*, and *it* are gender-specific. The reason God is referred to as "He" is not that He is male; rather, there are no pronouns that are applicable. Consequently, He, capitalized, refers to God.

There was a great children's TV program called *Schoolhouse Rock* that taught kids with song. Two wonderful songs explained classifications of words and parts of speech. "A Noun Is a Person, Place, or Thing," written by Lynn Ahrens, clearly stated that which we all know. In fact, we use the word *thing* in place of a name with astonishing regularity.

No one, however—*no one*—calls God a "thing" or "my thing."

"Verb: That's What's Happening," a song by Bob Dorough, could actually be about God.

Following are two appropriate stanzas:

> I get my thing in action (Verb!)
> In being (Verb!)
> In doing (Verb!)
> In saying
> A verb expresses action,
> being, or state of being
> A verb makes a statement
> Yeah, a verb tells it like it is! (Verb! That's what's happening)

> # God asked Moses
> # Do You Know My Name?
> # I am known by My Deeds

God asked Moses,
"Do you wish to know my name?
I am known by deeds!"
Deeds require actions. Only verbs.
Acts of kindness are verbs, not nouns.
Creation is a noun that implies a verb.

The following definition is given in *Webster's Dictionary*:

> **create**
> verb: to make or produce (something): to cause (something new) to exist: to cause (a particular situation) to exist: to produce (something new, such as a work of art) by using your talents and imagination

When we consider the attributes of God, none of them is a noun. God is the action. God creates. The limitations are in our languages and in our comprehension.

> And God created man in His image; in the image of God He created him; male and female He created them. (Genesis 1: 27)

Image did not mean physical image, as God is not physical in any context. The specific word does not exist yet. God said, "I shall be as I shall be." God did. God does. God will do. God is the action.

SELAH IN THE TITLE

Stop! Think intently!

The title *God Is a Verb* was the context for this book. Then, suddenly, I found the title was taken. It has an ISBN number.

Oops!

The new title was almost instantaneous: *Selah!* Selah was already a major section of this book. It is found most often in Psalms. I was taught that selah means "stop and think about it," and that is my definition.

As a teenager, I often used Psalm 143 as my prayer. It contains the word selah, and saying *selah* was as important to me as *amen*. I paid particular to all the Psalms that contained the word. Thus, it has had particular significance to me all these decades.

When I read the word *selah*, I instantly stop and think with dedication and intensity. To me, it is an indication of strategic importance. It is an emphasis and a call to be repeated. Did you hear what I said? Do you understand why I said it and what it means? What does it mean to you? How does it fit your context? Is it the same as mine? Be clear about this before you proceed. Do not forget! Reflect!

It comes most often after the statement or verse. It is akin to a command. Pay attention to this aspect specifically and with the intent to understand.

However, an Aish rabbi gave this explanation: The Talmud (Eruvin 54a) says that selah means "forever." The Radak (twelfth-century France) saw it as a musical notation for the singers to raise their voices. And Ibn Ezra (twelfth- century Spain) understood it to mean "true and certain."

Finally, Rabbi S. R. Hirsch, in nineteenth-century Germany, explained that, typically, selah remains "untranslated" because it has no intrinsic meaning. Rather, it is poetic and adds extra emphasis, like someone yelling, "Yahoo!" in joyous emotion.

According to Wikipedia, selah means:

1. Amen (Hebrew: "so be it") in that it stresses the truth and importance of the preceding passage;
2. this interpretation is consistent with the meaning of the Semitic root ṣ-l-ḥ also reflected in Arabic cognate salih (variously "valid" [in the logical sense of "truth- preserving"], "honest," and "righteous").
3. Alternatively, selah may mean "forever," as it does in some places in the liturgy (notably the second to last blessing of the Amidah).
4. Another interpretation claims that selah comes from the primary Hebrew root word selah (סָ,הָל), which means "to hang," and by implication to measure (weigh)

This book accepts these viewpoints and definitions of selah from Wikipedia. There was no declared definition in the times of the Psalms.

The perfect quality is that it is most applicable to a verb. The clearest term is *valid*.

The idea of measuring is interesting, as it is a directive to get high-quality data in your assessment. The intention is to consider the aspects carefully, with precision—in other words, to reflect and study with attention to detail.

Selah is actually an exclamation and emphasis. There is a passion about this word, and in using it, as cited earlier, Rabbi Hirsch said that it has "no intrinsic meaning." In that case, it is somewhat like "hallelujah." In our usage, there is a deeper and wider definition to selah than has hallelujah.

Remember, every single word in Psalms connects back to the Torah. All were written in the context that "Torah is truth" We are taught that if you do not understand any statement in the Torah as truth, keep studying it until you understand the truth.

Therefore, selah implies reconsidering and reflecting back to the source, to the Torah, particularly the book of Genesis. As mentioned, there is no declared definition from the times of the Psalms. It was commonly understood. It connects to the realization that every verse in the Torah is explained by the next two verses.

Selah is properly said at the end of a phrase or concept. Stop and think with verve! This is valid and important.

Selah!

Reconsider and repeat it with passion and verve
It refers to a verb!
God is a verb—It's valid
Consider it,
and celebrate with verve

HIS NAME

'Tis but thy name that is my enemy.
Thou art thyself, though not a Montague. What's Montague? it is nor hand, nor foot, Nor arm, nor face, nor any other part Belonging to man. O, be some other name! What's in a name? That which we call a rose By any other name would smell as sweet.
So Romeo would, were he not Romeo call'd, Retain that dear perfection which he owes Without that title. Romeo, doff thy name; And for that name, which is no part of thee, Take all myself.

—William Shakespeare
Romeo and Juliet (II, ii, 1–2)

What is the proper term for God, a verb? Verbs do not have a pronoun: he, she, or it. Nouns often have gender-specific qualities, but God, a verb, does not have gender. We refer to God as He, capitalized, to differentiate from the pronouns. As such, He does not have gender indications unless someone attempts to make an issue.

In common usage, God, capitalized, does not refer to a male human being.

God, capitalized, refers to the one and only supreme intelligence, not any gods of human manifestation.

We can and certainly will continue to discuss or indicate "God."

We each have a general concept of what each of us means. *He*, capitalized, is used as the name for similar universal references. While few agree on who or what we call *God*, we all understand that we are talking about the same universal presence. To use *She* as a substitute for *He* creates miscommunication by instilling gender-identity considerations. *He* does not have a gender. The lowercased *he* is absolutely gender-specific.

The presence and gender aspects of God are indicated twice in the Torah. In the garden of Eden, the sweet, feminine voice of God, called the Shekinah, talked directly to Adam and Eve. At Mount Sinai, when delivering the first two commandments, God spoke in a thunderous voice that was unbearably loud. Readers generally consider this voice as masculine. As these are the only times of direct interaction with God, we facetiously could call Him "The Voice." That term has already been copyrighted globally in many languages for a media enterprise. It specifically has no sacred connotations.

In Hebrew, there are seventy-two names for God. One name, *Yud he vauv he*, is too sacred to be uttered. The solution for Jews is to call God *HaShem*, which means "the name." HaShem wisely resolves the issue, as "the name" supersedes nomenclature and categorization.

While the name HaShem resolves the problem for the Jews, who have the same tradition, it is awkward and without meaning for most others. It also is without relevance in and for the tree of knowledge of good and evil.

The common names, therefore, are limited to *God* and *He*, regardless of whether someone is thinking about God as a noun or God as a verb.

El is one of the 72 names for God in Hebrew

El is the name for God meaning strength, might or power. The basic form "El" appears 250 times in the Tanahk, which is essentially the Old Testament other than the Torah or the first five books.

IN THE BEGINNING

The God Idea in Jewish Tradition by Rabbi Israel Konowitz was cited by Elie Wiesel: "Anyone willing to deepen their knowledge of the Jewish tradition's concept of God and His role in history should read this book which combines erudition and wisdom." It is an awe-inspiring book to say the least. The ninety chapter titles in themselves are a knowledge base of subjects about God Himself.

The title of chapter 1 is "Who is God and What is His Name?" The Pentateuch begins with the words, "In the beginning (*bereshit* in Hebrew) God created …" (Genesis 1:1). Why was the world created with the letter *bet* (the first letter of the word bereshit)? Why was it not created with *alef* (the first letter of the Hebrew alphabet)? The reason is that the letter bet has two points, one pointing upward and one downward and to the back of the letter.

bet

If one asks the bet, "Who created you?" the first point indicates upward, implying, "He who is above created me."

"And what is His name?"

The second points backward and says, "The Lord Adonai is His name."

This is a critical concept for this book. God began with the letter bet. This letter contains two points, a pair. They are similar and equal. Thus, God created with equilibrium and harmony, first of all. A pair of points show that God did not create a hierarchy.

God created a harmonious and unified system—one letter with two points, rather than an alef, which stands alone. Our universe is based on pairs in equilibrium. Without doubt, our planet and our people were created with the same intention and action.

Opposites and hierarchy are of human origin and consideration.

God created in pairs that always are in balance.

If God created in harmony, how did God enable the free-will choice of humans to exist? God *retracted* ever so slightly. That space, where God does not exist, is the location for our free-will.

One of the many aspects of this information is that the letter alef implies oneness. It is first and alone. It could signify God, who is the ultimate oneness. This even beginning creation, with the dual points in the letter bet, signifies the pattern we observe continually.

One is divided or becomes two—a pair, always a pair. God continually creates in pairs: two separate but aligned aspects. We must always work to see the pairs work in harmony and balance, not separation and opposition. (Konowitz, I)

Rabbi Konowitz went on to quote the Rav "The world was created using ten attributes: wisdom, understanding, knowledge, strength, power, rebuke, justice, judgement, mercy, and understanding." "'Wisdom is defined in classical Judaic sources as assimilating information from other sources: "Understanding" means the ability to deduce one matter from another, and "knowledge" refers especially saintly individuals are vouchsafed by Divine inspiration. (Konowitz)

Was one of Rabbi Konowitz's topics "God as a Verb," you might ask? He thought in Hebrew. He would have not have concerned himself with mundane parts of speech in English. However, in English, the predicate adjective completes the verb and describes the subject..

Without question, one is in awe of the level of awareness and clarity that Rabbi Konowitz had with God.

RATIONALE

Rationale is a set of reasons or logic that are the basis for a course of actions or beliefs. This book has some basic principles and concepts that I, as the author, use to support the reasoning that God is a verb. This chapter reflects my reasoning so that my point of view need not be a deterrent but rather a path to communication. My information is not frivolous. It may not be customary for many people, but I hope you will consider whether you question my assertion or my data. I invite a discussion about both, but please know whether it is about God or about my rationale. I look at the discussion to be about pairs of thoughts, not opposites.

Some clarification is needed.

In human consideration, time is measured by our planet rotating around the sun. A rotation takes twenty-four hours—from sunrise to sunrise, for example. In our vocabulary, *day* refers to that rotation. Uncapitalized day. That would be a nanosecond in God's calculations. God's *Day* is probably an eon. An eon is considered to be about a billion years. For the sake of comprehension, God is *He*, capitalized. His Day is *Day*, capitalized.

Second, I regularly refer to Torah in this book. Torah is the first five books of the Jewish bible, the Tanach, often called the Pentateuch. It was an oral tradition for hundreds of years, but the main characters lived for centuries. Shem, the son of Adam and Eve, lived until the time of Abraham. There were people who recalled, with acute memories. My acceptance of that story is based largely on the long and vital life of Sarai bas Asher, who lived for thousands of years and was able to recall, almost a thousand years later, crossing the Red Sea when the waters parted.

The stories in Genesis were a living oral history, a very accurate oral record.

According to the oral history of the Jews, there were seventy-two rabbis, six from each of the twelve tribes of Israel, who were called to translate Torah. The miracle was that all seventy-two produced essentially the same document. There are but six letters that are under question.

Torah is a holy document, written in perfection, that no human being could have designed.

As a student of Torah, I noticed that each verse was followed by two that explain it. This is evident throughout all five books. This is the pattern I find in all God does. One is followed by or divided into a pair—a complementary pair, aimed at equilibrium. God never creates division into opposites, which are always separate from each other. The separation is always directly against balance and truth.

bet lamed

Torah ends with the letter l and starts with b. Right to left

Thus *lab*—meaning soul, heart, authority within, love—is an endless cycle from God containing only truth and love.

> Hear, O Israel: the LORD our God, the LORD is one. And thou shalt love the LORD thy God with all thy heart, and with all thy soul, and with all thy might. (Deuteronomy 6:4–5)

In the Hebrew text, the word *heart* is in the center of the text for verse 5. It is the proper context for these last and first letters of Torah. It means a heart that understands knowledge. Thus, it can be comprehended as inner truth and knowingness.

If you do not understand that it is about truth, study it until you do. If you do not understand that God has been trying to teach us to be kind to each other and grateful to Him, go back and study it until you get it. It is a perfect document. The customary phase is, "Torah is truth."

If you cannot comprehend Torah as truth, I strongly suggest you study it until you comprehend every word as truth. An immense number of very intelligent people have paved the way to understanding. I read many things as coming from an exasperated God.

The first of the five books of Torah is Genesis, or Bereshit/Bereshis. This is the story from the garden of Eden through Abraham. It is the book that is imperative for all peoples. Genesis contains the first three covenants between God and humans on this planet to enable His plan for the garden of Eden.

The four other books apply to Jews as a nation, specifically. Their story is the tree of life. It was dormant in the garden of Eden until Jews accepted Torah from God at Mount Sinai. Every person on this planet is connected to Genesis and the tree of knowledge, the way of return. All can study the other four books in the context of Genesis for their own guidance.

The remainder of the Tanakh, which is largely similar to the Old Testament, is all written by Jews in the context of Torah as truth.

Every thought refers back to Torah for understanding and clarity. Some of the Tehillim, or Psalms, are written in the pattern of Torah. These are by Moses or King David, to the best of my knowledge. They followed the pattern, but it is a matter of a few verses, not the entirety.

Jesus taught the way of return. He was, in my understanding, the first person who taught the concept of the tree of knowledge as the path upward to God. Once I could get beyond the concepts of the Council of Nicaea in the year 315 CE, I could recognize what Jesus taught. (That is the subject of another book, *One Century, Twelve Jews*.) Please understand that I believe Jesus taught Torah devotedly. He did not change Jewish beliefs whatsoever. He was a gregarious, devout student at Beit Hillel, while Hillel the Elder, a Jewish sage and scholar, was still alive. Jesus was not an

Essene. He was an activist, not a scholar. He was the first person to teach the tree of knowledge, and he taught action, not study. When you consider Jesus and his teaching, he was definitely concentrating on God as a verb.

There is a good commentary in the Jewish Virtual Library about Jesus. When I began working with a Torah-based project, the biggest upset for me was the distortion of time and events in the New Testament. Read James, the brother of Jesus and the only book written by a practicing, observant Orthodox Jew who knew Jesus. The qualifying terms are most obviously added in the Council of Nicaea. You can read through the lines that the brethren were secularized Jews.

Understanding Jesus from the point of view that he taught the way of return led me to understand that all true prophets receive *from* God, aligned on the tree of life. However, they teach the return. All teach the tree of knowledge, one way or another.

Consequently, I wrote this book for those who have strong opinions, one way or another. It is a context to consider. It may well serve to spark a discussion among the millennials, many of whom are atheists.

Look at this concept as a way of pairing the concepts of God, rather than those who think they have the only way. There is no single path back to God. We all have our own soul journeys upward. We need all the knowledge and all the pairing possible. This book is intended to provide clarity and understanding, based on concepts in Genesis, particularly the garden of Eden. Once we have an intelligent basis for life on this planet, with historical continuity, we can begin the process of alignment to the Age of Aquarius and think in harmony and brotherhood of all humankind.

Our lives are designed for our own personal return to God, in harmony with others.

AHA!

God can create anything—from the tiniest entities to the most huge and complex. It all is orderly and intelligent. There is, however, an exception.

Angels and archangels and other heavenly beings follow their instructions and purpose unconditionally. They do not have choice.

In God's universe, the missing element, free-will choice, must come from others.

That is the purpose of human beings on our planet earth. We must choose to be kind and grateful to God and to our fellow human beings.

Angels are incredibly happy in doing whatever God needs and wants. It is their purpose. From all we know, they always follow their purpose, whether it's a one-time event or a continuum for long periods. When they succeed, both God and the angels are happy, but it was a mission, not a choice.

God lacked humans coming to him out of free will, in gratitude or in being kind to other human beings. It was flat.

Somehow, sharing hard times is important, but, if necessary, we can manage hard times when alone. The difficult part is to be alone when we have great news or a great event or circumstance, without someone with whom to share it and respond. It is the commonality of joy that matters. God could not create a joyful reaction to Him.

He tried civilization after civilization on our planet, hoping they would be grateful. Civilization after civilization failed totally. There was no bond of joy, gratitude, or thanksgiving. It could be understood as a long-term chess game, where it was about wits, or a dollhouse, wherein God would move the dolls here and there.

Shared joy and appreciation were missing. God destroyed many civilizations in trying to achieve a partnership of God's creating and the people responding in awe, appreciation, wonder, and kindness to each other.

He wanted humans to love each other and to be nice. He had many failures, such as Lemuria and Atlantis. Currently, a dozen ruins from a dozen prehistoric destroyed civilizations have been identified. God kept starting over to no avail.

Then, God had a huge *aha*!

Humans needed a free-will choice to leave, in order to have a free-will choice to return. They could not be expected to return if they never made the choice to leave.

God then developed a plan for the garden of Eden, Adam, and Eve. They would have perfect conditions. There was only one rule; a very simple rule with no ambiguity: do not eat from the tree of knowledge of good and bad. That meant knowledge of everything in between good and evil.

> And the Lord God commanded man, saying, "Of every tree of the garden you may freely eat. But of the Tree of Knowledge of good and evil you shall not eat of it, for on the day that you eat thereof, you shall surely die." (Genesis 2:16–17)

What if humans had to have the tree of knowledge of all things *before* they had moral rectitude?

As obedient, bucolic beings, they did not have the awareness to understand the scope of things, right or wrong. It would be analogous to your favorite pet making moral decisions without knowledge.

In this case, Adam and Eve did not *want* knowledge; they got it. Only then could they understand their previous actions.

The order of events of Adam and Eve were as follows:

1. God gave a dire warning to two simplistic human beings.
2. They did not pay attention to the warning. Without any serious or thoughtful consideration, they ate the apples.
3. They received the tree of knowledge of all things.
4. They then had the tools for reason, logic, understanding, wisdom, and kindness. They became sentient beings.
5. It is human beings who have identified eating the apple as a sin. It is impossible to think that God, who is positive and purposeful and kind, set up people as those whose first act was to sin.
6. The positive, purposeful plan was to establish free-will choice, with the entire range of knowledge available to all.

What if the original sin is a human interpretation?

The first mistake was, in fact, a very good choice. They left with knowledge of good and evil and everything in between. God put the plan into action 5,783 years ago. It is a 6,000-year plan. How are we doing?

Aha! -- an exclamation properly followed by an exclamation mark, is one of the great, unappreciated and deliciously nuanced words in the English language.(Safire, W.)

WHY AND HOW?

From the ancient teachings, we learn two essential aspects:

- A positive, purposeful God created everything.
- The purpose of human beings on our planet is to live eternally in a joyous circle of God's creating and our gratitude.

God has no negative aspects whatsoever. He does not create anything or do anything that is not positive. If you are in doubt about any act or idea of God that is not clearly wonderful, think until you understand. Any aspect that is less than good is a limitation of our capacity to understand. If God is everywhere and can create anything, how did He create the possibility for humans to have a free-will choice to return?

This is the most critical question! God retracted ever so slightly, and in that space is the space for a free-will choice. In that space, there is the possibility for humans to have their free-will choice to return to God in awe and appreciation.

There are no imperfections or incompleteness in God's work on this planet. The capacity for humans to live in an open, stable, harmonious system is the limitation. It isn't God. It is us.

Humans seem to create the separation from unity and clarity. The drive is away from harmony and toward hierarchy, which is the absolute separation from God. Humans have not created sufficient paths of awareness, clarity, and kindness. Many religious leaders are separatists and are hierarchical. Many more have taught a righteous return, one way or another. Find a teacher who thrives on compassion and balance and awareness, not on ego or elite concepts.

CHOOSING THE TREE OF KNOWLEDGE

When He put Adam in the garden of Eden, God gave very clear instructions. There was no question of the instructions being vague. No one could ever come back and say, "I did not understand the rule." No one could say, "I made a mistake," or "*You* made a mistake," or "I didn't think it mattered." God did not say, "This is a sin," or "You will be punished."

Then, Eve was created, and together, they chose to eat the apple. They risked their lives.

Knowledge implies understanding of good and bad as choices and the ability to discern the differences and similarities of the spectrum between them. There are no secrets. The range is all-encompassing. Knowledge implies using our intelligence and the factors available to us, such as experience, learning, and interacting with others during the process of life itself. The tree of knowledge is knowledge without limits; knowledge without bounds.

The significant aspect of the tree of knowledge is that it was the choice for a meaningful life, based on possibilities. In the garden of Eden, all was provided, and there were no obvious opportunities for personal growth. The tree of knowledge requires one's thoughts and active participation in one's own life. They were bucolic. They were not sentient in anyway.

The challenges of a life on the tree of knowledge with differentiation and distinctions, with possibilities, is far different from that of angels, who do their missions happily and dutifully. The angels do not have the joy of making decisions and improving matters for themselves and others. Do they have heartfelt gratitude to God for giving them a good task? Since the garden of Eden, humans have the full range of opportunities to create a meaningful life with kindness and gratitude.

We can live using the attributes God has and has made available for us. Within the garden of Eden, they might have had a perpetual childhood and innocence.

Was it really a bad choice to choose knowledge? Was it a bad choice to follow their curiosity? Was it a bad choice to make the huge decision together? Did they have to make their choice on the first day?

It is quite possible that if Adam and Eve had not chosen to eat the apple, their children most certainly would have. Then, there would have been all sorts of complications. Their children would have disobeyed their parents as well as God. God could have started over once again, since his covenant with Noah had not happened.

The two apple trees were the test. Then, they became the metaphor for the patterns, the organizing system. This system, recognized in *God Is a Verb*, is not complicated. It connects back to King Solomon's temple and Pythagoras. It is a framework for organizing concepts, whether they are sacred or not.

Any data can be put into the system. It is a relationship model that enables a person to evaluate and organize data.

Hopefully, having an organizing system and basic universal concepts will enable a respectful and comprehensible dialogue from both similar and dissimilar stances on morals, philosophy, and religion. The way of return is dedicated to the ability to look at things that are seemingly different and to find the similarities. Likewise, one can see the differences and find common ground.

TWO TREES IN THE GARDEN OF EDEN

The Tree of Life and the Tree of Knowledge

In the book of Genesis, or Bereshis, the rule and the actions established the tree of knowledge and the way of return for all peoples. The tree of life was fallow until the Jews, as a nation, accepted the Ten Commandments.

> And HaShem said: 'Shall I hide from Abraham that which I am doing; seeing that Abraham shall surely become a great and mighty nation, and all the nations of the earth shall be blessed in him. (Genesis 18:17–18)

Most religions since Abraham have believed in *one supreme God*, whether stated directly or not. All teach some form of the Golden Rule—to treat people with kindness and consideration—at the core of their beliefs. Three covenants in the book of Genesis/Bereshis established the tree of knowledge and the way of return for all peoples on our planet.

Adam and Eve chose to leave the garden of Eden. It was their free-will choice, and they took with them the gift of the tree of knowledge—knowledge without limits—for every person on this planet, regardless of their recognition of the process of return. The entire purpose of this

6,000-year plan is to return to God, with awe and appreciation of God and our fellow human beings. We do not proceed blindly, as the first things Adam and Eve received were the gifts of sight and awareness.

Genesis contains the stories that enable us to return to God, with knowledge and applied values. The stories can be read with positive, purposeful meaning.

Meanwhile, the tree of life lay dormant in the garden of Eden. Nothing happened with it throughout the entire book of Genesis.

Virtually every religion and teaching has the Golden Rule as a core component of their concepts. Jesus attended Beit Hillel while Hillel the Elder was still alive; Jesus's primary teacher was one of the great holy rabbis.

Hillel taught, "That which is distasteful to you, do not do to another."

Jesus taught, "Do unto others as you would have them do unto you."

Their versions are a perfect example of pairing.

Eastern religions have similar teachings, with an implied return to higher consciousness. The principles are consistent with the tree of knowledge. The stories of the garden of Eden and the deluge are found globally.

Consider that every human being has his or her own beam of light connected to God as source. There is no right way to honor God and each other. It is everyone's free-will choice to find his or her own perfect path. The choices, as to details, are ours. God clearly has given choices for an ethical choice for us all. There is no one religion or path that is better. Every single beam of light is a perfect manifestation of our connection to God. How we live is a direction of our own souls. It is always—*always*—about pairing and harmony, leading to peace on our planet. We must follow our hearts, our minds, and, most of all, our souls, our innermost beings, to treat God and others the very best we can.

The beam of light and life that we all have connects to our souls, our images, our connections, and our awareness to higher consciousness and God, as a verb.

Aspects of the Two Trees

My son, forget not my teaching;
But let thy heart keep my commandments;

For length of days, and years of life,
And peace, will they add to thee.
Let not kindness and truth forsake thee;
Bind them about thy neck, write them upon the table of
thy heart;
So shalt thou find grace and good favour
In the sight of God and man.
Trust in the LORD with all thy heart,
And lean not upon thine own understanding.
In all thy ways acknowledge Him,
And He will direct thy paths.
Be not wise in thine own eyes;
Fear the LORD, and depart from evil;
It shall be health to thy navel,
And marrow to thy bones.
Honour the LORD with thy substance,
And with the first-fruits of all thine increase;
So shall thy barns be filled with plenty,
And thy vats shall overflow with new wine.
My son, despise not the chastening of the LORD,
Neither spurn thou His correction;
For whom the LORD loveth He correcteth,
Even as a father the son in whom he delighteth.
Happy is the man that findeth wisdom,
And the man that obtaineth understanding.
For the merchandise of it is better than the merchandise
of silver,
And the gain thereof than fine gold.
She is more precious than rubies;
And all the things thou canst desire are not to be compared
unto her.
Length of days is in her right hand;
In her left hand are riches and honour.
Her ways are ways of pleasantness,
And all her paths are peace.
She is a tree of life to them that lay hold upon her,

And happy is every one that holdest her fast.
The LORD by wisdom founded the earth;
By understanding He established the heavens.
By His knowledge the depths were broken up,
And the skies drop down the dew.
My son, let not them depart from thine eyes;
Keep sound wisdom and discretion;
So shall they be life unto thy soul,
And grace to thy neck.
Then shalt thou walk in thy way securely,
And thou shalt not dash thy foot.
When thou liest down, thou shalt not be afraid;
Yea, thou shalt lie down, and thy sleep shall be sweet.
Be not afraid of sudden terror,
Neither of the destruction of the wicked, when it cometh;
For the LORD will be thy confidence,
And will keep thy foot from being caught.
Withhold not good from him to whom it is due,
When it is in the power of thy hand to do it.
Say not unto thy neighbour: 'Go, and come again,
And to-morrow I will give'; when thou hast it by thee.
Devise not evil against thy neighbour,
Seeing he dwelleth securely by thee.
Strive not with a man without cause,
If he have done thee no harm.
Envy thou not the man of violence,
And choose none of his ways.
For the perverse is an abomination to the LORD;
But His counsel is with the upright.
The curse of the LORD is in the house of the wicked;
But He blesseth the habitation of the righteous.
If it concerneth the scorners, He scorneth them,
But unto the humble He giveth grace.
The wise shall inherit honour;
But as for the fools, they carry away shame. (Proverbs 3:1–35)

FIRST COVENANT: ADAM AND EVE

God devised a plan for Adam and Eve to leave the garden of Eden by choice. He created a perfectly beautiful garden with everything they could need. He gave Adam one very simple rule: "Do not eat the apple from the Tree of Knowledge" (Genesis 2:16–17).

Then God created Eve. She and Adam quickly justified eating the apple and did so.

Then, the feminine voice of God, the Shekinah, very softly spoke to them in a nonthreatening way.

They could have approached God with some humility and asked for forgiveness. They could have asked for a second chance. They did not. They didn't even try to save each other.

They broke the rule. They had caused each other to do wrong, and they blamed each other. They lied. They obviously did not respect God.

God banished them.

This was His first judicial act. God is merciful. He did not kill them, as they had been warned. He banished them.

This was, in fact, what He expected. It was what He wanted. There was no ambiguity. He had the clear and certain conditions for a free-will choice to return to God in gratitude and acts of goodness.

This was very straightforward.

What do we know about the tree of knowledge? First of all, Adam and Eve suddenly could think about what they saw. Instantly, they realized their bodies were different, and they clothed themselves. It was the first aspect of awareness. It was not about good or evil but rather a visual truth. Before they had knowledge Adam and Eve obviously were unaware. They couldn't reason, and they saw nothing. They had no experience.

It was no surprise to God that they ate an apple from the tree of knowledge. They literally knew nothing. They had not been tested, and they had not learned. The idea of having good advice or discussing it with God did not even register as a possibility.

When God gave knowledge, it was based on recognizing information. It was not a case of declaring opposites but of realizing a pair of different-looking bodies. The tree of knowledge contains everything in between good and evil. It is knowledge without limits. It provides the conditions to create awareness and harmony, not opposite poles. Humans choose to make opposition and controversy, rather than looking for peace.

Our planet is not about separating everything according to the North and South Poles but knowing everything in between, with the purpose of informed choices.

Those who have raised children know that one of their first actions is to disobey, just to prove themselves. My granddaughter was not yet two years old when she made her first stance for independence. She ran up the driveway away from me. I took a photograph, since it was so purposeful. She got to the end of the driveway and stopped. She knew her own limits. She had more awareness than Adam and Eve. She had knowledge and knew right from wrong immediately.

God giving Adam and Eve the admonition not to partake of the apple of knowledge was the mindset of a parent with small children. There is that stage when a toddler declares his or her independence of thought, word, and deed. Adam and Eve were at that stage, as they were just formed, knew nothing, and had no experience. They could have been permanently in that state of being, without knowledge or forethought. They choose to take a path that was based on making good choices. Their first choice was not good. The first covenant with Adam and Eve ended with these words:

> And God said: 'Behold, the man has become as one of us, to know good and evil; and now, lest he put forth his hand, and take also of the tree of life, and eat, and live forever.' (Genesis 3:22)

God clearly established that Adam and Eve permanently had the tree of knowledge of good and evil. Adam and Eve and all peoples on our planet have knowledge as part of our being. There are no limits to our knowledge. This is indicated by including both good and evil and everything in between. As always, God creates in pairs with the potential for harmony. He does not limit our knowledge.

We all learn to use our senses, our minds, and our experiences to live meaningful lives. We all have the potential to have knowledge as the basis for our entire lives. We can learn from the past and the present and have an informed future. Access to knowledge and the ability to use it is our gift. The way we use it is our decision.

Furthermore, He does not limit the access to the tree of life. It stood idle until the covenant with the Jews as a nation. It was always guarded for protection from damage, but it has been ours to understand as a reference for the tree of knowledge.

Adam and Eve and all descendants have been given every aspect possible to help them on their way of return. There are no restrictions on that which we receive and use. There are no limitations on our minds and experiences. We all have the potential for a free-will choice to return to God with gratitude and acts of kindness.

Adam and Eve chose to leave the garden by their own volition. They did not even consider the potential for wisdom, implied by the tree of life. The free-will choice to leave enabled a free-will choice to return. Together, they chose to eat of the tree of knowledge.

SECOND COVENANT: NOAH

God wanted humans to have a level playing field for the return. He wanted to eliminate problems of genetics, stories, and enemies stemming from people from prior civilizations. In addition, there had been virtually no progress from the descendants of Adam and Eve.

As time went by, there was no progress toward a return to God, based on kindness and gratitude. There was little intention to be nice to others.

Noah, however, was doing well with his family. God assigned Noah the task of building a huge boat on the top of a mountain. The purpose was to save Noah and his family and sets of animals.

Noah even had to lug trees past the tree line because the mountain was high. It took 120 years. The entire time, Noah's neighbors jeered at him. Noah trusted God, as it didn't make sense. It was a tough job, and the neighbors' jeering made it worse.

Finally, Noah gathered his family and all the animals, and the deluge came. As we know, it rained hard for forty days. It covered the mountain.

The surprising thing to Noah was that he missed all the folks who had taunted him. He did not like the void in companionship. He asked God never to destroy people again. "Please, don't give up on people."

God agreed.

God sent the sign of a dove. He has kept His word.

It must have been very tempting at times to get rid of everybody and start again. We can all note times when God could have decided to just scrub this experiment. He had numerous times, before the covenant with Adam and Eve, when He destroyed civilizations. God also sent the Pleiades, the cluster of stars that are the basis of astronomy, as well as the calendar still in use today. One of the number sets is seven. This corresponded to the days counted in Genesis.

While Noah offered this covenant to God, there is every reason to think that God knew from previous civilizations that there would be reasons to get rid of everyone. At this point, we need help to save our planet and our civilization.

God has never wavered, as we know.

THIRD COVENANT: ABRAHAM

Over the centuries, the population spread, but there was considerable paganism, worshipping many gods, animals, and things. The whole purpose for humans on planet earth was to have a thriving return to God. There was idolatry everywhere, but no one showed gratitude to God. It was time for a demonstration of respect and appreciation and trust of God, the one, true, positive compassionate God.

The man at the highest level was Abraham. God chose Abraham to show his loyalty and trust of God. It seems there were sacrifices of all manner at that point. They were made to all manner of animals, gods, objects, a very large number of things—*nouns.*

It was time for drastic proof that God was the one, true, absolute God. *Whoa!*

Abraham was asked to sacrifice his beloved son, Isaac. Isaac agreed.

There are endless interpretations regarding this covenant. Consider this story with respect to God is a verb and that God always creates in pairs, not opposites. First of all, they both knew. The story of the great heroism to follow God unquestioningly was agreed upon and carried out by both father and son. Second, it tested them at the core of their beings. They were tested at their essential natures.

Abraham was tested in his compassion and Isaac in his integrity. They were tested as a pair, and they succeeded together. While there is no way to really understand the reason this was proof to God of their undeviating gratitude and respect for God, we do understand God's response—unwavering loyalty to Abraham and Isaac, which continues.

There was another trip up a mountain to connect with God. Isaac was bound and about to be killed. All of a sudden, a small goat appeared. In the nick of time, it became the "scapegoat," a substitute for Isaac.

Being willing to make this sacrifice was proof enough for God that there could be monotheism on this planet. Abraham was promised as many descendants as there were stars in the sky.

FOURTH COVENANT: THE COVENANT WITH THE JEWS

The Ten Commandments

In God's determination to have the garden of Eden trial succeed on planet earth, He had one further critical element to put in place. In the Garden of Eden, Adam and Eve ate an apple from the Tree of Knowledge of good and evil. Thus, the way of return for everyone is aligned to that tree. Each person on this planet is required to make his or her own positive choices in the return to God, in awe and appreciation, in doing acts of kindness, and in showing respect for God.

One might imagine God as a source of light and love, emitting a beam of light to each of us—a ray of sunshine to all people so they have their own direct connections to God. We all have the potential to freely choose our paths and keep our own lights shining.

God decided that He must have a stream that separately comes down through a group of people who will have pledged their children, throughout eternity, to live according to God's rules. The purpose was to have an orderly, intelligent, universal, complete, positive, enduring, organizing system. It had to enable free-will choice and be flexible as well as stable..It had to be singular and without debate. That could not happen by chance.

The first covenant established free-will choice. The second established the significance of relatedness. Abraham and Jacob accepted the Master, highest intelligence and leader, we call God. The fourth covenant established the system itself with a group dedicated to maintaining and living the system. There was an agreed- upon Covenant at Mount Sinai with the Nation Of Isreal, the Jews..

Descendants of Isaac most likely were chosen because of his willingness to be sacrificed to the one true God. This pattern of two trees is the fundamental aspect of God's plan to have humans return in a free-will choice. The significant aspect that is overlooked is that the two trees actually comprise a double helix of a pair of trees. The trees contain a similar but not exact formation and have different streams, or sources of data and stories.

In Jacob's dream, he actually envisioned the angels ascending and descending on the ladder while he wrestled with the negative force. His dream depicted the double helix of the two trees. There were two streams, two directions, connected to God. Thus, the two trees in the garden of Eden were established as a system on our planet earth.

Many centuries later, after enslavement in Egypt and time in the desert, Jews were led to Mount Sinai to hear God. *Led* is a gentle word. Actually, God held a mountain over their heads. The Jews had to promise to give their children to God in order to receive His Word.

There had to be a permanent, stable group, or nation, to receive God's Word unconditionally. Within the covenant, they had free will, but it required absolute allegiance to Torah, the five books, and to doing acts of kindness, as directed by God. Thus, they live the tree of life. As a nation, they are bound to receive from God His instructions and mandates.

What happened to those Jews who left the covenant? They left by their own choice. Logically, they became aligned to all others on the tree of knowledge of good and evil.

The fourth covenant establishes the plan, created in the garden of Eden, as the operating system for people on our planet. Jews, as a nation, accepted the Ten Commandments. These are the rules, as given by God, to create a living model through every generation. By adhering to God's guidebook, Jews connect the tree of life to planet earth.

There is no indication that any attempt, before the garden of Eden, established a cogent ethical system on our planet. The four covenants, the five books, established the organizing system for all the people on this planet.

The two trees establish a pair, which are designed to enable an ethical system on this planet. Both are positive, and both are necessary. This pair is totally consistent with the ways God has established a free return to God in positive, purposeful acts by all.

TWO TREES: TWO DIRECTIONS

God created two trees in the garden of Eden; they have become the analogy for the operating system of our planet. It is a double helix, an organized, open, stable system for all the peoples on our planet. The purpose is to live freely and compassionately with each other and to be thankful to God.

There are many ways of return. There have been many prophets. Arguably, every prophet who is aligned to the way of return has received instructions and information through the tree of life. They receive *from* God and teach the way of return *to* God. All teach some form of the Golden Rule. Thinking that one is better than another is a miscalculation and a separation from the double helix and, most of all, from God and our purpose for being.

The concept of knowledge of good and bad actually means knowledge without limits. It includes everything between good and bad. God does not create opposites. This is a pair that is inclusive.

It is up to all people individually to make the choice for themselves on values and information.

It is important to understand that Jesus, a religious observant Jew who was passionate and gregarious, taught the way of return to secularized Jews. The primary teachings we have from him directly are the Beatitudes.

He taught Torah with simplicity and accuracy and studied at Beit Hillel. He did not add to or change Torah. As previously mentioned, Jesus was an activist, not a scholar. He may well have been the first person who taught the way of return on the tree of knowledge.

Many ways of return now are established or personal. They have the Golden Rule in common, in one form or another. Most have a concept of the supreme-intelligence Creator. It is the alignment to the tree of knowledge of good and evil that Adam and Eve freely chose.

Were there communities that predated the garden of Eden? If any remain, they have been peacemakers and have not spread their teachings beyond their communities. They have always lived on the way of return.

The critical verse is Genesis 18:18: "All the nations of the world shall be blessed in him."

This clearly establishes a way of return for all peoples. Most religions have had a prophet who believed in one supreme God and have taught some form of the Golden Rule and gratitude. Consider that every human has his or her own beam of light connected to God. There is no "right" way to honor God and each other. It is everyone's choice to find his or her own perfect path. The choices as to details are ours. God clearly has given choices for an ethical life for all.

The tree of life, however, was not put actively in place until Mount Sinai, when the Jews, as a nation, agreed to abide directly by the Word of God.

> And out of the ground made the LORD God to grow
> every tree that is pleasant to the sight, and good for food;
> the tree of life also in the midst of the garden, and the tree
> of the knowledge of good and evil. (Genesis 2:9)

To make this clear: the tree of knowledge was identified specifically for Adam, Eve, and all people to adhere to thereafter. It is as a nation. It was Jews, as a group.

The two directions of the two trees was started with one direction, one tree, when Adam and Eve were banished. It was the Tree of Knowledge. The second tree, the Tree of Life, was instigated as a result of the covenant at Mount Sinai. The Tree of Life descends.

Abraham established one God for all his generations. Muslims are conscious of the tree of knowledge. His descendants—through Hagar, Ketura, Esau, and other children—are all Gentiles and follow the tree of knowledge, the way of return.

Because of their vow, descendants of Jacob established the tree of life. It came into action long after the tree of knowledge of good and evil. It was lying fallow until the nation Israel was formed by their accepting the Ten Commandments and pledging their children throughout every generation.

It is a matter of pairs, not a hierarchy, on our planet. God is supreme, and He works with pairs in creation. The nation of Israel is not better or worse than Gentiles. It is a mandatory component of the return to God on our planet and for all peoples. Both trees are necessary. God has created an open, stable design for the human beings on our planet. There are two trees, and they operate as a double helix—compatible but in the opposite direction. Once again, the two trees were designed as a pair. It means knowledge without limits on the tree of knowledge. Specialized knowledge including aspects of relatedness is included in the tree of life, according to the fourth covenant. They are a pair to establish peace on our planet. Both are necessary.

The binding of Isaac in the book of Genesis solidly placed the tree of knowledge of good and bad on our planet. It is an organizing system for the free-will choice to return to God. No other teachings exist that predate this process. If a fragment of teachings is ever found, it would be useful for study, but it made no impact on the last 5,783 years.

During the entire period of Genesis, the tree of life lay dormant. The gates protected the garden, and it was open to all, but no one came. God, as is consistent with all God does, had a plan.

It was, of course, two trees. The plan was to have the tree of knowledge as the basis for the return to God, with a free-will choice for kindness and gratitude. The tree of life was coming *from* God as an eternal source of kindness and order.

In effect, the tree of life comes *down* from God directly, and the tree of knowledge is the return *to* God.

The next four books of Torah are the story of putting the tree of life in action through the nation of Jews. The story—from Isaac to the giving of the Ten Commandments and the last day of Moses's life—is decisively about Jews, as a nation, accepting this system. They pledged their descendants through eternity. The rules are specifically to live according to the tree of life. All the teachings are available to all.

Jews, however, live it as a system with dedication. They receive the instructions from God. There is no debate. This can be understood as God designing and creating in complementary pairs. They are designed to be in equilibrium. Individuals may choose to leave, thus living according to the Tree of Knowledge. It is the element of Jews as an eternal collective dynamic that is the distinguishing factor.

Jews receive.

The tree of life comes down.

Gentiles return.

The tree of knowledge goes up.

REPETITION AND RATIFICATION

God teaches us through patterns and through repetition. There is every indication that if we do not properly understand our priorities and our lessons, we will repeat them, quite possibly for many lifetimes. It likely will be with the same soul groups or families. Same lesson. Over and over. As a family historian, I have seen patterns in my family in this lifetime that parallel those in generations before.

The pattern of the two verses regarding the two trees in Genesis is very clear. One verse is a whole, followed by a verse of concept that is dual. The same pattern is in the first two commandments. The whole of Torah, the five books, is written entirely with the same pattern. Each verse is followed by the next two verses as an explanation or consideration. The pattern is analogous.

The verses in Genesis 2:16–17 are a set.

The first verse states the garden as whole.

The second is specific, regarding the tree of knowledge of good and evil.

The second verse has two connected concepts: good and evil.

The pattern of the two trees and the symbology of the two trees correspond directly.

These two verses are critical to understanding Torah, which was written in a perfect mathematical sequence. Each verse is explained by the following two verses. Anyone can check the meaning just by following the pattern—each and every time. It is beyond the capability of human minds to conceive of such geometric patterns, much less achieve them.

It is a sign of God's connection to us through His holy Word.

God's giving of the first two commandments audibly is a congruent pattern. The first commandment is followed by one that has two parts.

First commandment:

> I am the Lord, your God, Who took you out of the land of Egypt, out of the house of bondage. (Exodus 20:2)

Second commandment:

> You shall not have the gods of others in My presence. You shall not make for yourself a graven image or any likeness which is in the heavens above, which is on the earth below, or which is in the water beneath the earth. (Exodus 20:3–6)

The process parallels cell division. One separates into two.

There are variations in the results.

They are pairs, designed to work in harmony, not opposition. We learn from this pattern of the two trees and the second commandment that creation was division into pairs, not opposites.

Opposites are an extreme differentiation of pairs. Opposites are not the general rule and are difficult to achieve. Polarization requires intention and dedication to achieve. Denial of the opposite requires rigid determination. Distinctions, similarities, and commonalities are the function of the two trees.

Good and *evil* can be either polar opposites or a pair that includes knowledge of everything in between.

Twos show differentiation.

Pairs cooperate, unify, collaborate, and look for commonality, partnerships, and togetherness. We and our.

Opposites separate, divide, are hierarchical, and maintain their individuality and distinctions—adamantly!

They are "*apart*ners." *You and me* are clear.

The relationship of two joining or dividing determines all other connections.

The most basic aspect is ego. Does your ego dominate and differentiate in your decisions and actions?

Polarization largely is the result of ego.

"Apartner" words polarize.

- positive—negative
- good—bad
- right—wrong
- mine—yours
- best—worst

Is the comparison from ego and judgment or is it from balance and harmony?

Together is a wonderful distinction.

Self-focused cults are particularly dedicated to apartner concepts. They limit knowledge and understanding in their passion to always state an affirmation of mental attributes. They specifically do not allow high-quality data or information or experience.

"You are telling me a story," a minister told me. "Stop it! I will pray for you, but you must never call me again."

I wanted a resolution that was critical. Instead, I received an "affirmation" by rote. They are, in reality, mental manipulations. Clearly, they reject biblical tales and moral tales.

In their cases, saying, "There are two sides to everything," means they are totally polarized and never make a responsible decision. They are regularly very hurtful indeed. They are never appropriate. Realistically, anyone can see they eliminate contacts and communication outside of their own control group. They deny intelligence in their interactions.

We learn from scientists that any computation based on insufficient data is always faulty. People who do not allow sufficient high-quality life have no way to make any decision or statement that is not egocentric. The unbelievable concept that there are two sides to everything is passionately against God, who is truth. If you do not know and do not care about determining truth, you always have an extreme void in data and experience and, most of all, truth.

These ego-focused people are controlling and dictatorial, and they create extreme negativity by never allowing our hearts, minds, and instincts to deal with circumstances and information that is paramount to being appropriate. They are hugely separated from the way of return. They have no concept of it.

Actually, they can never be useful to God because they only tell God what they want. They do not listen to God or to others.

Their "affirmations" are the best example of being *off* the way of return. I think of my interactions with these folks and realize they have the ultimate self-vested interest priorities.

They have no humility. They never consider, "Is this nice?"

Ego-focused people are the penultimate apartners. They are the icon of separation.

The actuality is that anyone who thinks there is but one way to God is an apartner. Anyone demanding his or her own religion for others is the most clearly separated from God. Fortunately, our founding fathers recognized the danger of religious mandates and created our Constitution with a dedication against church and state. They were quite adamant in excluding the practices in Europe.

There are problems with those who have low self-esteem—I am addressing only situations I have personally observed for an extended time. They have clearly demonstrated the reverse of ego-dominant people. In these cases, the people have intense idol worship. They are totally subservient to their idols and exhibit no attributes connected to their own souls. They choose idols, who have aggrandized egos. The intensity of their idolatry is astonishing.

Resolution and rectification of all kinds are the essence of "pair" thinking, rather than opposites. These acts of kindness are critical in the way of return. We all have a litany of phrases that cause instant separation; these phrases certainly do not need to be elucidated.

Healing words lead to pairs and pairing, not apartners and opposites. For example:

- I'm sorry.
- I didn't think.
- I never thought.
- I didn't know.
- It never occurred to me.
- Tell me what happened.
- Tell me what you think.
- What can I do to help?
- What do your children need?
- What do you need?

The list of soft words with kind thoughts is endless. Every word matters. The intention matters.

There is a wonderful Japanese teaching: *Seicho No Ie*. One of their teachings is to always repeat *thank you*.

"Arigato. Arigato gozaimas."

"Thank you. Thank you very much."

People understand this to a magnified degree.

They pay attention.

Children learn this well.

The same policy works for an apology. "I'm sorry. I'm really very sorry."

From the reaction I received from the Japanese when they heard "Arigato gozaimas," I would suppose that learning to say thank-you in other languages is a wonderful way to be on the way of return— easily! Repeating the phrase is an immediate positive connection. In the Hawaiian language, *aloha* means affection, peace, compassion, and mercy. Nowadays, it is also used for *hello* and *goodbye*. It is, perhaps, the best word for the way of return.

Say it often.

Another example of the importance of ratification is saying *amen* after a prayer. Amen locks it into a higher zone. "This is important! Hear me!"

A woman was told in a spiritual experience that God needed her to be useful to Him. It would be harder than she thought and take longer than she thought, and she wouldn't understand it, even if she were told. With her attitude, she would do it anyway. It would require her to release her free will in some specific circumstances, so she would have to make a vow with a ritual to affirm her agreement. She was asked what she wanted in return (to bring honor to her parents and their ancestors and to facilitate their descendants for three generations). She could break her vow at any time. The mandate was to make another vow with a ritual to break the first vow.

Never, ever forget to break a vow properly. I include that admonition very seriously. Do we consider the extremely important aspect of breaking a vow at all? It appears this could be an aspect that we overlook in general. It is easy to rectify this, once you realize the significance.

If you make a vow, renewing it is a good practice, but ending it properly is essential. Divorce is a common occurrence that began with a vow, but it is not ended in respect of the vow.

It is easy enough to follow that practice, on the possibility that it is a mandate.

THE FIRST TWO COMMANDMENTS

As lists go, the Ten Commandments are essentially universal. Yet from the written word of the Bible, there is no agreement as to what they are. Jews, Catholics, and Protestants are totally committed to their own versions.

The significant differences in the different versions are the first two commandments. Given that God gives us information in patterns and repetition, these two commandments show the clear and certain differences in the tree of life and the way of return.

God gave the first two commandments directly to the Jews in the process of their becoming a nation. God delivered these two commandments in a thundering voice that frightened the Jews to the core of their beings. There were two million Jews there, and God's message and purpose was quite clear. God communicated verbally and directly. Arguably, nothing else has mattered more to that extent.

They had centuries of hard slavery, the plagues, and wandering through the desert, and now they pledged their children for eternity to hear this. It was unbearably loud, thundering beyond anything we can imagine. The other commandments were communicated by Moses. There is no doubt as to God's intention to make certain these two commandments were a unit, separate and distinct.

The differences between the Jews and the Christians are not the words but how they are communicated and placed in the set of ten.

One of God's primary patterns is to divide one into a pair of two. The two are always separate but equal. They are created as a set for unity and equilibrium. God never creates opposites. Humans create opposites.

There is no doubt that these two commandments were delivered in exactly this manner with this intent. This is the pattern for the tree of life. Arguably, the tree of life, which had been resting in the garden of Eden, was activated by God's delivering these two commandments.

Throughout Torah, every verse is in this pattern of one explained by the next two.This is a major aspect of Torah. Do not dismiss it!

The Jews were there and probably were overwhelmed by the intensity and volume of God's voice. God adamantly presented Himself so there would never be a question about His authenticity. *Know who I am!* It is a complete thought and provides the context for all that follows.

The first commandment is the announcement. The connection to God is unequivocal. . The second commandment has two paired statements, two parts in alignment, . This combination is evident throughout Torah. This far beyond the capability of any human being. The other pattern, as noted, is the entire format of Torah—as one verse followed by two as indicators. It is the basic pattern of creation.

	Jewish
1	I am the Lord your G-d who has taken you out of the land of Egypt.
2	You shall have no other gods but me. You shall not make for yourself any graven image,
3	You shall not take the name of the Lord your G-d in vain.
4	You shall remember the Sabbath and keep it Holy.
5	Honor your mother and father.
6	You shall not murder.
7	You shall not commit adultery.
8	You shall not steal.
9	You shall not bear false witness.
10	You shall not covet anything that belongs to your neighbor.

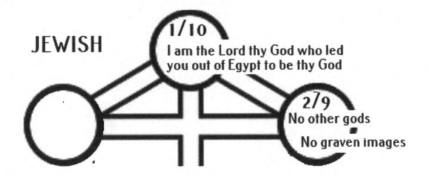

JEWISH

1/10
I am the Lord thy God who led you out of Egypt to be thy God

2/9
No other gods
No graven images

Following are the Catholic and Protestant versions of these two commandments. The order makes no sense unless you are on the tree. The Tree of Knowledge ascents on the same order, which were given to the Jews long after Adam and Eve began Life on the Tree of Knowledge of All Things. They had no experience or understanding. They had a free will choice. They had the potential to Return to God through Awe, Gratitude, Self- Awareness and Relatedness as they progressed upward toward higher consciousness and God.

The ascent is applicable to all peoples on this planet. It is possible to observe this pattern through Prophets through the Ages. They apparently all experience the Trees coming down, but the teach the Way of Return, knowingly this pattern or not.

	Catholic	Protestant
10	I, the Lord, am your God. You shall not have other gods besides me.	You shall have no other gods but me.
9	You shall not take the name of the Lord, your God, in vain.	You shall not make unto you any graven images.
8	Remember to keep holy the Lord's Day.	You shall not take the name of the Lord your God in vain.
7	Honor your father and your mother.	You shall remember the Sabbath and keep it Holy.
6	You shall not kill.	Honor your mother and father.
5	You shall not commit adultery.	You shall not murder.
4	You shall not steal.	You shall not commit adultery.
3	You shall not bear false witness.	You shall not steal.
2	You shall not covet your neighbor's wife.	You shall not bear false witness.
1	You shall not covet your neighbor's goods.	You shall not covet anything that belongs to your neighbor.

In the Catholic version the first commandment includes the first part of the pair. God does not work in that manner. God starts with one and divides it into two—a pair. This pattern starts with two.

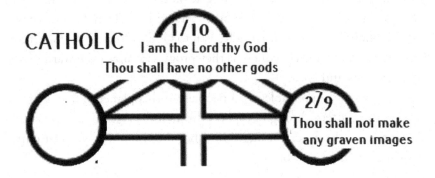

In the Protestant version, the first commandment is eliminated and the second becomes two separate commandments.

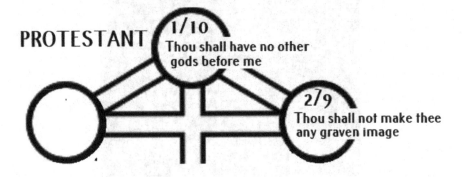

Both the Catholic and Protestant versions are perfectly aligned with the tree of knowledge for the way of return. There is an organized format designed as a counter-parallel system to the tree of life. Every person must create his or her own way of return. It is an individual, free-will, voluntary process. The tree of knowledge of good and bad can be used at will. It is, of course, knowledge of all manner of things.

It can be noted that our calendar, which was given to Noah, according to the Dead Sea scrolls, Makes sense in the Tree of Knowledge ascending. The First seven attributes are deemed achievable by most people. We can cite the days of the week from Monday in the first position up to Sunday in the seventh. Appropriately, the term in Hebrew, which is used in this book is Chesed, which means loving-kindness. It is an excellent tern for our Sunday card.

This book uses the Protestant version since God or higher consciousness or the Supreme Architect as the Freemasons apply or Buddhists infer, is above the Tree of Knowledge for all people.

The seven day week with the Sabbath makes absolute sense on the Tree of Knowledge. The number seven represents the aspects aligned to the tree are achievable by all peoples ascending. The higher three components are comprehensible, but not always achievable by people in general. This tree begins with the individual and the personal return to God in awe and appreciation.

Tree of Knowledge

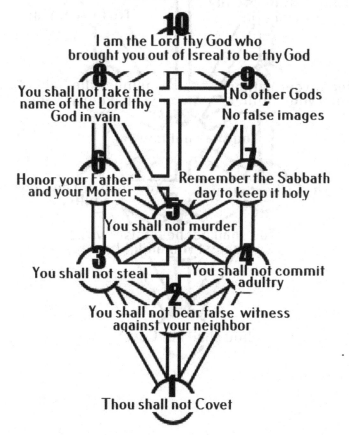

10
I am the Lord thy God who brought you out of Isreal to be thy God

8
You shall not take the name of the Lord thy God in vain

9
No other Gods
No false images

6
Honor your Father and your Mother

7
Remember the Sabbath day to keep it holy

5
You shall not murder

3
You shall not steal

4
You shall not commit adultry

2
You shall not bear false witness against your neighbor

1
Thou shall not Covet

One would assume the Hebrew Calendar is connected to the Tree of Life. It is based on a nineteen year cycle, which is not known to this author.

The Tree of Life descend into the whole of Klal Israel as a group.

The important distinction is that the commandments on both trees refer to actions. The commandments refer to verbs. We connect to the higher realms through deeds.

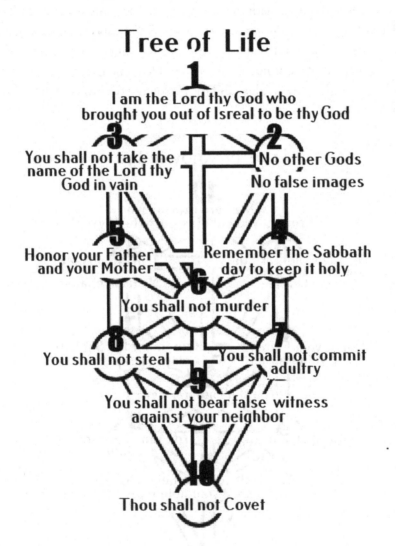

Tree of Life

1
I am the Lord thy God who brought you out of Isreal to be thy God

3
You shall not take the name of the Lord thy God in vain

2
No other Gods
No false images

5
Honor your Father and your Mother

4
Remember the Sabbath day to keep it holy

6
You shall not murder

8
You shall not steal

7
You shall not commit adultry

9
You shall not bear false witness against your neighbor

10
Thou shall not Covet

How might we consider Islam and the Ten Commandments in alignment with the Tree of Knowledge?

In Arabic, the word "Allah" means "The One who deserves all worship."

Previous editions of the book have had very positive responses from Muslims. I have had strong feelings that Mohammad taught the Tree of Knowledge Ascending. Islam accepts the Book of Genesis as source. However, there has been no avenue for inclusion until I found a study which I have abstracted:

The Ten Commandments in Islam By Abu Amina Elias

The closest single passage in similarity to the Ten Commandments occurs in the chapter of the cattle (*surat al-an'am*). In this passage, many of these biblical commandments are restated, with a heavy emphasis on fulfilling the rights of Allah and the rights of people.

Allah said: Say: Come and I will recite what your Lord has forbidden for you, that you not associate anything with Him, and be good to parents. Do not kill your children out of poverty, for We will provide for you and them. Do not approach lewdness, whether it is public or private. Do not kill the soul which Allah has made sacred except by right of justice. This He has instructed you that you may reason. Do not approach the property of the orphans, except in a way that is best, until he reaches maturity. Give full measure and weight in justice. We do not charge any soul except within its capability. When you testify, be just even if it concerns a relative, and fulfill the covenant of Allah. This He has instructed you that you may remember. And this is My straight path, so follow it and do not follow other ways, lest you be separated from His way. This He has instructed you that you will be righteous. Surat al-An'am 6:151-153

With this in mind, we find that the parallel sayings to the Ten Commandments are conveyed all throughout the Quran and Sunnah. The following are some prominent instances in which Muslims are instructed to uphold these teachings:

First commandment: You shall have no other gods before Me.

Allah said:Your God is one God. There is no God but him, the Gracious, the Merciful Surat al-Baqarah 2:163 Say: I am only a man like you to whom it has been revealed that your God is one God, so take a straight path to him and seek his forgiveness. Surat Fussilat 41:6

Second commandment: You shall not make idols.

Allah said:Do not call upon another god alongside Allah. There is no God but him. Everything will perish but his countenance. Judgment belongs to him, and to him you will return. Surat al-Qasas 28:88
Forefathers, for which Allah has not revealed any authority. They follow nothing but assumption and what their souls desire, yet there has already come to them guidance from their Lord. Surat al-Najm 53:23

Third commandment: You shall not take the name of the Lord your God in vain.

Allah said:Unto Allah belong the best names, so call upon him by them and leave those who violate the sanctity of his names. Surat al-A'raf 7:180 And Allah said: When you see those who engage in offensive discourse concerning Our verses, then turn away from them until they engage in another conversion. Surat al-An'am 6:68

Fourth commandment: Remember the Sabbath day and keep it holy.

Allah said: O you who believe, when the prayer is announced on Friday, then proceed to the remembrance of Allah and leave trade. That is better for you, if you only knew. Surat al-Jumu'ah 62:9

Fifth commandment: Honor your father and your mother.

Allah said: Worship Allah and associate nothing with him, and be good to parents and relatives. Surat al-Nisa 4:36

Sixth commandment: You shall not murder.

Allah said: The believers are those who do not call upon another god alongside Allah or kill the soul which Allah has made sacred except by right of justice. Surat al-Furqan 25:68 The killer is not a believer while he is killing. Source: Ṣaḥīḥ al-Bukhārī 6809, Grade: *Sahih*

Seventh commandment: You shall not commit adultery.

Allah said: Do not approach unlawful sexual intercourse. Verily, it is immoral and an evil way. Surah al-Isra 17:32 The adulterer is not a believer while he is committing adultery. Source: Ṣaḥīḥ al-Bukhārī 2343, Grade: *Muttafaqun Alayhi*

Eighth commandment: You shall not steal.

Allah said: Do not consume the wealth of each other in falsehood. The thief is not a believer while he is stealing. The plunderer is not a believer while he is plundering and the people are watching him. Source: Ṣaḥīḥ al-Bukhārī2343, Grade: *Muttafaqun Alayhi*

Ninth commandment: You shall not bear false witness against your neighbor.

Allah said: يَاO you who believe, fear Allah and always speak the truth. Surat al-Ahzab 33:70 And Allah said: Verily, truthfulness leads to righteousness and righteousness leads to Paradise. A man may speak the truth until he is recorded with Allah as truthful. Verily, falsehood leads to wickedness and wickedness leads to the Hellfire. A man may tell lies until he is recorded with Allah as a liar. Source: Ṣaḥīḥ Muslim 2607, Grade: *Sahih*

Tenth commandment: You shall not covet.

Allah said: Do not hate each other, do not envy each other, do not turn away from each other, but rather be servants of Allah as brothers. Source: Ṣaḥīḥ Muslim 2559, Grade: *Sahih* Beware of envy, for it consumes good deeds just as fire consumes wood or grass. Source: Sunan Abī Dāwūd 4903, Grade: *Hasan*

As we can see, the Ten Commandments are entirely compatible with Islam and they are, in reality, the essence of all divine revelations. They can be the best point of departure for sharing Islam with Jews and Christians, and working together in fulfillment of our ethical obligations. (*Allah, and Allah knows best)(Elias,* Abu Amina)

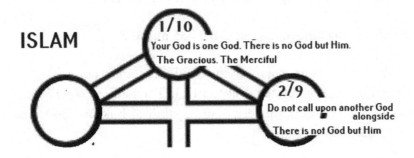

God is One. Perhaps the hardest concept for humans is to understand the oneness of God, the indivisible. The ten commandments can be seen as actions for each person to follow in increasing awareness to that which is beyond our limitations.

Applying this list to the Tree of Knowledge Ascending, a case can be made that it embodies and orderly system that allows free-will choice based on actions and verbs. It is aligned to our souls and our positive, purposeful deeds being a Return to God and higher consciousness. God always creates in pairs, not opposites.

Thus, all three Abrahamic Religious streams can be understood in terms of the Tree of Knowledge in Genesis and from the ten commandments in Deuteronomy. These are actions, not nouns. They provide an orderly system for humans on our planet.

Perhaps Jews incorporate both Trees as a unified whole system.

Christianity and Islam are conceptualized as the Ascent in the Tree of Knowledge, Every human being begins with their own awareness, followed by relationships. These are key to all other actions.

PATTERNS

As Bob Dorough wrote in *Schoolhouse Rock*,

> Three is a magic number.
> The past and the present and the future.
> Faith and Hope and Charity,
> The heart and the brain and the body,
> Give you three as a magic number.
> It takes three legs to make a tripod
> Or to make a table stand.
> It takes three wheels to make a vehicle
> Called a tricycle.
> Every triangle has three corners,
> Every triangle has three sides,
> No more, no less.
> You don't have to guess.
> When it's three, you can see
> It's a magic number.

Patterns Begin With Three

\Until there are three, there is no form, no pattern.
Once is happenstance, twice is a coincidence, three is a
pattern.
Once is a dot.
Twice is a line.
Three times are a shape, a pattern.

God—a verb, with infinite oneness, with no boundaries and no parts—has no patterns.

God creates patterns.

God creates in an infinite number of patterns. The patterns begin with three aspects.

In a lecture, Bucky Fuller showed how stable a triangle is. He had a four-sided model with movable corners. Indeed, they could be shifted all sorts of ways. Triangles were a major aspect of his work, including the geodesic dome.

Patterns beyond those having three aspects go on with more numbers, but three is the very basic form and set—a design. Three dots can make a pattern but not one. Two go every which way but cannot create a stable pattern or form. Two dots connected make one line. This is extremely elementary but essential in recognizing God in action.

We go one with four to make a shape with dimensions and then on to time. The important aspect of time is that it is not at all linear. It exists in cycles and circles.

The two trees are integrated, orderly, intelligent systems. They are multifaceted and multidimensional. They coordinate sets of data into a comprehensible relationship model. They can be spheres, helixes, or a two-dimensional drawing.

Bucky Fuller taught that triangles are the building blocks of the universe. Certainly, his work shows that concept repeatedly.

In APOD (astronomy picture of the day) from NASA, there was a drawing of the neutron bounce, the tiniest component known. I cite this design in particular, as it is so very important in the tree of life and the tree of knowledge. It is about the patterns, the building blocks

Are triangles, with their rigid structure, the reason our universe does not collapse?

The patterns, the organizing system, for *God Is a Verb* is not complicated. It connects back to King Solomon's temple and Pythagoras. It is a framework for organizing concepts, whether they are sacred or not.

Any data can be put into the system. It is a relationship model that enables a person to evaluate and organize data.

Hopefully, having an organizing system and basic universal concepts will enable a respectful and comprehensible dialogue from both similar and dissimilar stances on morals, philosophy, and religion. The way of return is dedicated to the ability of looking at things that are seemingly different and finding the similarities. Likewise, one can see the differences and find common ground.

The tree of knowledge, the tree of life, and the double tree are depicted as follows. The format is a perfect organizing system and can be used for all manner of data. The ancient diagrams are included, as there are numerous references to these patterns.

TIME

There are many ways to measure time, but other than measuring with a calendar, time is nonlinear. It is always in cycles, goes forward, and connects to the past.

The first aspect of time is found in Genesis and the days it took God to create components of our universe and of our planet, specifically. One day of twenty-four hours makes no sense, cosmologically. It is a matter of understanding distinctions. A Day, capitalized, is eons long. A day, uncapitalized, is twenty-four hours. Both apply to periods of time without clarification.

Torah itself is written without linear order. It will not make sense until you recognize you are connecting situations and circumstances.

There are an endless number of cycles in God's universe.

There are a few that are of interest in this book.

The Mayan calendar is valid, yet the civilization is long gone and along with it, all continuity for that civilization going forward into our time. It speaks to the concept that God gave up on peoples until this 2,000-year experiment, wherein the people choose to leave. Therefore, a valid return is enabled. All of us observe cycles of the sun in a year, a week, or a month. We observe cycles of the moon as well. There are innumerable cycles. All have meaning.

A simple cycle is found in the relationship between the sun and moon. It takes nineteen years for the sun and moon to be in exactly the same relationship. Thus, for each of us, a new cycle begins every nineteen years. It is easy to chart your life in this pattern. It works very well in many ways. This is the core of the Hebrew calendar.

Our standard calendar was given to Noah after the covenant. There are fifty-two weeks of seven days, totaling 364 days. New Year's Eve is a separate set of thirty hours, dividing each year.

Native Americans look at cycles in an interesting manner. Imagine a circle, and when you break out of the circle, you must complete the entire circumference before reentering at the same place.

Jupiter has a twelve-year cycle around the sun, whereas the cycle of Venus is shorter than that of the earth. We see in astronomical data that they are at the same point about once a year. The significant qualification is that they are at the same point of longitude and latitude once in about two thousand years. When they are exactly aligned, the lamination is extraordinary. It is often explained by showing one candle exactly behind another. The light is magnified to a massive extreme. It happened in about 6 BCE. I believe that was the Star of Bethlehem. The three wise men were astrologers from the Far East.

The very next occurrence was in August 2005. It was the time of Hurricane Katrina, followed by another hurricane. Both made a right-angle turn—one to New Orleans; one to East Texas. Arguably, that was the onset of the Age of Aquarius. There are many theories. This is the one I accept at this point.

In defining the differences between the ages, the Piscean Age is depicted as two fish swimming in opposite directions. That is a remarkable icon, as concepts in the Piscean Age are always opposites and differences, rather than pairs and similarities, to create harmony. The Age of Aquarius is depicted with corresponding wavy lines. Reflect on this possibility. Selah.

Another aspect of the changing from the Age of Pisces into the Age of Aquarius is important.

There is an optical illusion as we see planets because of the shifts in the speed, motion, and relationship between planets and systems.

According to EarthSky.org,

> Astronomers use the term to refer to the occasional backwards motion of the planets as seen in Earth's sky. When used in this way, retrograde motion is entirely an illusion caused by the moving Earth passing the outer planets in their orbits. Meanwhile, real retrograde motions—of a planet's spin on its axis, of moons orbiting planets, and even of planets in distant solar systems—are a sign of long-forgotten collisions and captures. Real retrograde motion is one of the clues that astronomers use to piece together the history of our solar system, and the systems of other stars in our galaxy!

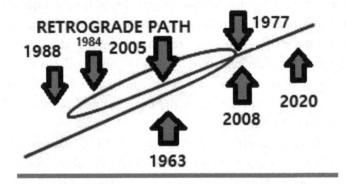

Possible timeline of entry into the Age of Aquarius: the initial entry into Aquarius was in 1963. It continued in Aquarius until 1977, when it reversed. May 1984 was the critical mass for peace, when 11 percent of the people were in consciousness for peace, and 1988 was the harmonic convergence. These were significant, paired events. The movement once again was forward. In 2005, the age moved into Aquarius for the next 2,000-year cycle. In 2008, we passed the farthest point in the initial entry. That marked the election of President Obama.

"Aquarius/Let the Sunshine In," one of the most iconic songs of all times, was introduced in the 1960s in the Broadway musical *Hair*. To many of us who came of age then, there are distinct similarities. The possibility that there was an entry into the Age of Aquarius that retrograded back into Pisces and came forth in 2005 is valid in this book.

Time is a tool for us to master in any number of ways. It exists, whether or not we make use of the knowledge.

God created an infinite number of patterns and cycles. Apparently, God never creates anything without reason, harmony, and connections. There is a reason for everything.

Humans make the errors in understanding and judgment. We have the choice to use time as a tool, just as we have the choice for using every other tool we have, in our knowledge without limits. The qualifier is always in recognizing the teacher.

VAULTING

The practice of vaulting is enhanced by recognizing cycles.

You can connect to previous times to recognize your patterns, as well as connecting to previous circumstances.

Vaulting is introduced as a concept for creating and furthering any new program or dynamic.

As a verb, the definitions of vaulting are:

1. to spring over an object, especially with the aid of a long pole or with the hands resting on the object
2. to do, achieve, or attain something as if by a leap

How Does This Work?

Your project is ready to start. You are in the gate, just like in the Kentucky Derby.

But wait! How far back are the roots of your work? How clear and clean is the trail to this time? You can go so much farther if you connect to previous affirmative roots and begin your approach from that basis. Jews can go back to Mount Sinai. It was a nation that accepted the tree of life as a system. It is encoded within Torah.

If you can clearly connect back to a point of time—the beginning, the origination of any person, concept, or activity—you create a pattern.

You create a dynamic that includes past, present, and future. It is a pattern of three. If you can connect back, you can establish the basis for a much stronger process. It is the set of three aspects that can propel a running leap into the future.

The trick is that you must have all issues resolved to get back to the beginning. Otherwise, you will found your process on an incomplete situation. It is the resolution that enables a healthy vault forward. Otherwise, you will be stuck in the muck and mire or proceed from a standstill.

Remember that patterns do not have to be physical. Patterns are evident in all our thoughts, words, deeds, and personal attributes.

Patterns are a priority. Look for similarities in things that seem different and differences in things that seem similar. Recognizing the distinctions in patterns makes a tremendous impact on all your choices.

Everyone else, including Jews who separated from the clan, must return on the tree of knowledge, whether they recognize it or not.

Stop! Look! Listen!

RELIGIONS AND PHILOSOPHIES

The Prophets and the Two Trees

We can understand Eastern spiritual teachings in the construct of the two trees. In every observable tradition, I have found a clear alignment. Prophets receive from God. They are not bound by the covenant with the Jews but rather the specific inspiration from God directly. They then teach a way of return to their followers. Thus, it is a corresponding, eternal, universal cycle.

Simplistically, many are paths for individuals to higher consciousness, to enlightenment. The values and traits, both similar and dissimilar, on their journeys can be diagrammed on the tree of knowledge. The concept of God as a verb can be aligned to their teachings.

Jesus and Muhammad

Jesus and Muhammad are the two primary prophets of the Age of Pisces; they clearly are in the Abrahamic traditions. They both taught the tree of knowledge and the way of return. Jesus, a Jew, taught secular Jews the tree of knowledge. Muhammad taught the tree of knowledge directly from Abraham.

The Pope and the Grand Imam

Historic Declaration of Peace, Freedom, Women's Rights

> In the document signed by Pope Francis and Ahmed el-Tayeb on Monday in the United Arab Emirates, the two leaders issue a strong condemnation of terrorism and violence: "God does not want his name to be used to terrorize people."

> The "Document on Human Fraternity for World Peace and Living Together" signed on Monday afternoon in Abu Dhabi by Pope Francis and the Grand Imama of Al-Azhar, Ahmad el-Tayeb, is not only a milestone in relations between Christianity and Islam but also represents a message with a strong impact on the international scene. In the preface, after affirming that "Faith leads a believer to see in the other a brother or sister to be supported and loved," this text is spoken of as a text "that has been given honest and serious thought," which invites "all persons who have faith in God and faith in human fraternity to unite and work together." (Tornielli 2018)

Indigenous Systems

There are maps of the languages in Africa and in North America. None of these languages and their roots contain reading, writing, and calendars. Do the rhythms and the chanting and dancing connect to nature and to a different aspect of God as a verb? There are no rules, no preaching.

Certainly, Black people have filled their churches with music of their own making, the source of which is their native heritage.

Native American powwows are also filled with chanting, dancing, and music-making. Their relationship to God is through verbs. Using the character of animals to illuminate aspects of their teachings is aligned to the concept that God is a verb. Certainly, animal spirits could be organized using the Tree of Knowledge.

Selah!

The wide diversity of spiritual quests, philosophical journeys, and believers and nonbelievers can be studied and comprehended using the tree of life as an organizing system. The ultimate purpose is to achieve enlightenment or universal intelligence. These can be understood in terms of God as a verb and the tree of knowledge. An invaluable process may be to diagram your own precepts in the format of the tree. Many Eastern teachings have common features that enable a comparison and, perhaps, increase understanding.

For those such as atheists and other nonbelievers, diagram your favorite quotes according to the tree. Diagram the values you respect. You might find that God as a verb is more comprehensible than is the denial of a master intelligence.

For many of us the problem with God is a matter of definitions. Understanding God as action of higher consciousness opens new avenues of wisdom and experience. It may be a closer concept for many teachings and experiences. It may cut through barriers of communication.

Many teachings do not define God or a god. They are focused on precepts, not the nouns. This is true for Eastern Religions, many ancient traditions as well as many spiritual endeavors coming forth and into the light. Identifiers and nouns decrease our understanding. Nouns by their nature limit.

God is a Verb and our souls are the image of of God, a verb.

THE FIRST RELIGIOUS CONTROVERSY IN AMERICA

In 1635, just fifteen years after the Pilgrims arrived in the New World, the Antinomian Controversy—a religious and political conflict—began in Boston. Importantly, it was only five years after the Puritans arrived. The two groups were not alike in many ways, particularly in religious concepts. The Pilgrims, living on the South Shore of Boston and on Cape Cod, did not get into this heated argument. They were a separate society.

The Antinomian Controversy began with the division regarding the Non-Separatists from Church of England and new religious thinkers, who wanted to eliminate religious laws . The fight was about whether one could receive the covenant of grace solely by one's beliefs or whether one had to follow the covenant of works and do acts of kindness.

Whether they recognized it or not, this actually was a battle as to whether God was a verb or not. Were verbs, which are actions, decisive in our relationship with God? God said to Moses, "Know me by my deeds." Likewise, we are known to God by our deeds.

Hutchinson and Wheelwright were connected by marriages as well as beliefs. He spoke at the Fast Day in 1637, which was intended to restore unity. He intensified the battle exponentially.

Ultimately, the issue was political rather than religious, as well as religious rather than spiritual.

The reality is that both aspects are part of spiritual living. Consciousness of a higher intelligence as well as the acts of kindness are the components of the Tree of Knowledge.

SELAH! SOULS

Our souls are in the image of God; our bodies are not. It is hard to comprehend God having a form. God is without boundaries or limits. This is the reason our souls need a container, a place where they can exist—in our bodies.

Our souls are totally aligned to the attributes of God. We are taught that souls were created before the acts of creating the physical components of the universe. They are eternal.

According to sixteenth-century rabbi and Jewish mystic Isaac Luria, souls can be divided and joined. The reasons God combines and separates souls all relate to the ultimate time when all of our souls can unite as one. Souls were created as one and then divided. Ultimately, they will join after the process of a return to God, in awe, appreciation, and kindness. It is our job to care for the well-being of our souls, particularly those in our own families—our soul groups.

At conception, a sperm and an egg are joined. The process of life begins. This pair, a sperm and an egg, are compatible, not opposites. They are the basic pair in human existence. As soon as they are joined, a body begins to form. It is the house for the soul—a noun in every way. The fetal heartbeat is a stage in preparing the body to receive and protect the soul. The fetal heartbeat happens months before the body is developed sufficiently to contain a soul, the breath of life. There are no spaces when the fetal heartbeat begins.

Around the seventh month, a new stage is reached—the brain is formed. The two hemispheres are a pair. They are separated by a space. It is the only place in the body that literally is a space. *Webster's 1828 Dictionary* provides an interesting perspective. Regarding the word *soul*, Webster is on the mark more than many people. One can see him readily adapting to the idea that a soul is a verb in the image of God.

soul

1. The spiritual, rational and immortal substance in man, which distinguishes him from brutes; that part of man which enables him to think and reason, and which renders him a subject of moral government. The immortality of the soul is a fundamental article of the Christian system. Such is the nature of the human soul that it must have a God, an object of supreme affection
2. The understanding; the intellectual principle. The eyes of our soul then only begin to see, when our bodily eye are closing.
3. Vital principle. Thou son, of this great world both eye and soul
4. Spirit; essence; chief part; as charity, the soul of all the virtues. Emotion is the soul of eloquence.
5. Life; animation principle or part; as, an able commander is the soul of an army.
6. Internal power. There is some soul of goodness in things evil.

mind

1. Intention; purpose; design. The sacrifice of the wicked is abomination; how much more, when he bringeth it with a wicked mind (Proverbs 21:27).
2. Inclination; will; desire; a sense much used, but expressing less than settled purpose; as in the common phrases, 'I wish to know your mind;' 'let me know your mind;' 'he had a mind to go;' 'he has a partner to his mind'
3. Opinion

Most of all, Webster recognizes the immense difference between the mind and the soul. He is quite clear about the attributes of a soul.

Then, Sigmund Freud, Carl Jung, and an incalculable number of others confronted the soul as part of the brain. It seems easily comprehensible that the "breath of life" goes into a location that God designed for it. It seems easily comprehensible that the "breath of life" was in the image of God. It is impossible to figure out how that is part of our brains.

Also, Freud would have known that there was an earlier meaning to the root word *psyche*, meaning "soul" as well as "butterfly." The soul is a liberated being. It flies. It is not bound by earthly restraints, not by the weight of the body or by gravity. When Freud's work was imported to this country, the word *psyche*, referring to soul, was translated to *mind*. (The German word for mind is *geistig* and bears no relation to the word psyche that Freud chose.) What Freud had intended as a spiritual quest became, instead, a medical methodology, and psychoanalysis lost its connection to its original concept of searching for one's soul. (Goldberg)

Once we understand that God is a verb, our souls—verbs—are liberated from our minds (nouns).

Our souls take flight from the limitations of physicality.

SELAH! EGOS

Voilà. As soon as our minds and our souls are separated in place and substance, our minds, located in our brains, have their own functions. The ultimate free will may have been that we are all in charge of the balance and interaction of our egos and our souls.

For the last twenty years, I have been in regular dialogue with a rabbi. He is adamant that there are "very, very, very few" instances in which problems between people are not caused by their egos. "Jealousy, lust, and ego destroy a person's life," he has said. Ego is the basis of all three.

Is my soul clashing with your ego? Are our souls in sync? If not, our egos are the problem because all souls connect to God. How many of the problems are caused by not understanding that our egos are in our brains and that our souls are in the space between the halves of our brain?

An aspect of human behavior is regularly outside of any pair and does not reflect back to God: *ego.*

Ego is your consciousness of your own identity. It is also defined as one's self, especially as distinct from the world and other selves. God does not have an ego. An ego is a human aspect and is not an attribute of God. It may be considered the human aspect most separated from God.

We must work to keep our own egos in balance. There is not one aspect of God that is commensurate with our egos.

Our souls and our egos should work in the aspect of pairs, but when they are not, most decidedly, they are opposites. Consider the possibility that all irresolvable issues are ego-centered.

Some teachings are entirely egocentric. It is quite probable that God does not even deal with egocentric issues. God does not have an ego, so this is a trait that is outside His realm. I have experienced teachings that deny data. They do affirmations or prayers that are strictly formatted, and they tell God what to do. That is mental manipulation. A truism is, "Affirmations based on ego are mental manipulations." It is not healthy for our minds. More than anything, these folks reject compassion. They will never resolve an issue because they love their mental gymnastics. They are taught that they are superior. That happens a lot with psychological venues. They are taught that their teaching is the only way.

They are wrong.

A very common characteristic in ego-dominant teachings and people is that they refuse to resolve any issue. It is never their fault. It is always their fault. It is a perfect hierarchical mindset.

It can be said that the ego is the location for our free will. It is the absence of God. Our souls are directly connected and aligned to God. This is the ultimate challenge. Bring your ego into harmony with your soul.

There is a truism: "Any computation based on insufficient data is always faulty." Egocentrism is invariably filled with insufficient and faulty data. It is a barrier to truth. An out-of-balance ego denies the rights of others and keeps only the priority of self.

A common teaching that is entirely based on ego is to turn the other cheek. It is not taught consistently with other Torah teachings. When anyone blocks resolution for another person, it is an act of extreme ego and cruelty. It only serves the ego of the doer, whether or not that person feels entitled. It also works when not accepting apologies. It is a supreme control characteristic. The ego person is in control of the other person or persons.

One group of ministers in my experience refuses data. They get into their canned affirmations. They never have understanding or compassion. In the end, they are the losers. Every unresolved issue that we face is incomplete. The denial of resolution is an aspect that we experience through the truth process at the end of life.

The denial of resolution is an ugly action in every way.

These same people are fond of saying, "There are two sides to everything." That does not mean they are both right. It takes sufficient high-quality experience and wisdom to ascertain truth and justice. Disregarding facts and compassion is a clear and certain separation from God and God's reason for creating us. Where there is division, the best solution is a willingness to forge a common understanding. The more data, experience, introspection, and awareness one has, the more possible it is to create balance.

A clue to the depth of separation into ego is how judgmental a person is. A clue toward resolution is to keep working until you get to truth. At least you will have attempted resolution. Truth does not have sides. Truth *is*.

Our souls and our egos are as close to opposite as possible. In fact, we could consider our egos as nouns and our souls as verbs. It is interesting that God does not have a corporeality or boundaries or an ego. God is a verb, and our souls are verbs. Our souls are in the image of God. Our egos may be the ultimate separation from God.

Putting those two aspects of our beings into harmony may be the ultimate challenge in our lives. Of course, we all need healthy egos. The problem is having an egocentric context that is way out of balance. It happens far too often. Are ego issues the test when we go through the truth process at the termination of our lives? Are our egos our legacies to our families? Is sociopathic behavior essentially an ego problem?

Interestingly, the first, primary, and essential attribute on the tree of knowledge for the way of return is self-awareness—that awareness of self and others. Ego is the absolute, clear, dominant factor as a failure to live with awareness. Ego prevents love, as it does not give.

A number of years ago there was a craze for teaching, "Look out for number one." They certainly were not thinking about God, who is number One, capitalized.

Reflecting on one's soul is the obvious method to get order over ego.

An objective on the way of return is to have clarity. Ego prevents clarity.

SELAH!

In 1948 the United Nations passed the Universal Declaration of Human Rights (UDHR), and in 2008, Karen Armstrong's Charter for Compassion was introduced globally. Both are important in bringing peace on this planet.

It is important to recognize that we are on the cusp of the Age of Aquarius. We may have entered this age during the 1960s for a short period and then reversed back into the Piscean Age. It was the "dawning of the Age of Aquarius."

When observing time in astronomy, there is an optical relationship, wherein periods and aspects reverse, called *retrograde*, into the preceding cycle. Since cycles are elliptical, it is possible to see this phenomenon on our planet. I observed this myself when leaving Grand Central Station in New York City on a train. Because of the differences in speed, a train on another track appears to be in reverse, yet both are going forward.

Christianity and Islam are both Piscean Age religions; they reflect this mindset. The two fish going in opposite directions show the dedication for opposites, which are hierarchical. It is now a glorious time to readjust to the basic concept of the Age of Aquarius, the universal brotherhood of humankind.

The concept I explain as *vaulting* is very important. We are in the process of entry into Aquarius. The organizing principle is to be able to connect back in time and thought before the Piscean Age, in order to shift into the Aquarian mindset cleanly.

It seems quite clear, when considering Hurricane Katrina, with the abrupt shift into New Orleans and then another into East Texas, that race relations are key, moving into Aquarius. The first president of the United States in the Age of Aquarius was Black; the second could have been a woman. A major presidential contender was focused on the principles of the brotherhood of man and was Jewish. It may have been easiest for him to get the principles that were predominant. Priorities have shifted dramatically.

The phenomenal upheaval at the onset of the Piscean Age seems to be repeating as we enter Aquarius. Hopefully, we can make the changes that are mandated.

THE LINWOOD
EXPERIENCE

Linwood Spiritual Center is on an extraordinary site in Rhinebeck, New York, with a view straight down the Hudson River. When it was given to the Sisters of Saint Ursula back in the 1960s, they first used it as a nursery and kindergarten for local children.

My doctor, whose kids went there, said, "My children come home every day singing happy songs." I enrolled my son immediately for the fall class. The children, their mothers, and the sisters were truly an idyllic group.

One of my favorite images was watching the entire group, with the sisters in their habits, as they ascended a hill so the children could meet cows. It was a happy time for all.

Yes, they did come home singing!

One of the activities was learning to count and sing in French as well as English. They knew the meaning of the songs. Great fun!

Years later, when my son was entering college, I visited Mother Mary Francis, the head of the order. She was eighty-nine years old at the time.

Instantly, she said, "Ah! Lance! I remember him well!" She went on to tell me stories about his playing with Scott, Andrew, Christopher, and others. She told me the games and activities that Lancer liked best with each of them. Amazing upon amazing!

She also remembered my daughter, Lael, who came two years later. Lael especially loved her classmates Elizabeth, Kate, and Bentley. Indeed! She even remembered that Kate and Bentley's brothers were Lancer's friends.

One day in kindergarten, Lancer asked me to buy a whole bunch of big balloons, saying, "Mother Mary Francis told us we could find God wherever there is air. I want God to have a place in my room!"

GOING FORTH INTO THE AGE OF AQUARIUS

The Two Trees, as Demonstrated by the Ages

Age of Taurus
> Both trees introduced

Age of Aries
> Tree of life activated by Jews
> Jacob's ladder

Age of Pisces

Tree of knowledge activated by Jesus, Muhammad, and others

Age of Aquarius
> The two trees operate as a whole system,

Remember to remember that the driving force for our souls is love that gives, the eternal circle.

God manifests kindness; humans reflect kindness in return. The Age of Aquarius is not the brotherhood of man. The new paradigm for the Age of Aquarius is aligned to God as a verb.

> # Aquarius: Humankind
> # Humans Being Kind

Age of Aquarius: Humankind. Humans being kind.

The Name for God, the Verb, is SELAH.
"EL" is one of the 72 names of God

When completing this book, it seemed that a term for God as a Verb, would be useful and appropriate. Having used the term Selah so often and knowing it has such a loose definition, it may fill a need for a distinguishing aspect of God.

THINKING IN THE PARADIGM: POEMS AND THOUGHTS

Grok It! God Is a Verb!

It is over the moon! There is a verb to describe, to "get" that God is a verb
Grok is a verb
To understand and empathize with something or someone to the extent that the object or person becomes part of one's sense self.
To empathize or communicate sympathetically; establish a rapport.
To understand, pay attention, and appreciate actively and profoundly,
To contemplate something or someone with full love and understanding,
To know completely and intuitively
To be conscious
To become one with.
To be

Groking is being
Let's grok! It!
Let's grok
on our souls as verbs
Grok it!
Rock it!
Lock it!

God Is a Verb!

God is a verb, a dynamic creative action, not the abstraction, but rather,
the doing and the being, the kind and the caring. The profound and the personal
Expansive, yet intimate,
Orderly, yet free
Constant, yet changing
God is the joy and brilliance of happening
The movement of the known and unknown
The mystery and the truth
Yes, God is a verb in constant action and love. God is the mastering of chaos, of static states, of disorder and disharmony
into a vast meaningful peace and harmony.

A Rose Is a Noun; God Is a Verb

A rose has a front. A rose has a back. God has neither a front nor a back.
God does not have corporeality. He has no body. He has no limits. Roses have substance. God does not.
Rather than thinking about God as a form
With the characteristics and quality of physical presence,
We shift to actions
To movement
To attributes of happening and being.

Once we realize God is not a noun,
We come to realize God is action. God creates.
God is a Verb.

Our body is a noun. Our soul is a verb in the image
of God
God is a verb, a dynamic creative action,
A positive purposeful force
Intelligence without form or constrictions
A vast array of traits and distinctions that radiate beauty
Beauty without physicality and dimensions
Compassion and kindness without limitations
All-knowing, yet intimate and personal
We experience God in our innermost thoughts and
feelings
Yet we constantly learn and know parts of the mystery
Beyond our comprehension
Our souls are the image, the component that is a clear
and radiant

Manifestation of God as a Verb

The very breath of life that makes us humans. Our bodies
are nouns that begin as a pair, a sperm and an egg join,
out of the millions of possibilities.
They join and grow into a noun, our bodies, our house
for our soul. God creates in pairs; our bodies are sets of
so many pairs.
Finally, after two trimesters, our brains, two halves are
ready
Two hemispheres with a space in the center
Right behind our eyes.

Spirit

the act of creating had to exist
as the beginning

there were no things in existence to create
ideas came before things
the void came before movement
before items and results
concepts preceded form
thoughts preceded words
words come to mind
ineffable
sublime
the soul
essence of creating
light
darkness
heat
cold
colors
numbers
time
souls
sound
Hebrew letters
Scientific principles
Space
Purpose
order out of chaos

Indigenous Peoples

From long-ago indigenous peoples until the present day, peoples have made a way of return to God through verbs, dance, song, chants, rhythm, music of all manner.

The *Mayflower* landed in Provincetown, before making their permanent home at Plymouth in December 1619. The Wampanoags, led by Chief Massasoit, determined the Pilgrims were not going to raid their villages and kidnap their people. They came for the Peace Pipe Ceremony. There were sixty braves in full regalia, chanting and dancing. It was their sacred ceremony. Our Pilgrims were baffled, to say the least. Ultimately, Chief Massasoit and Governor Carver smoked the peace pipe. This was apparently the first sacred ceremony in America between the native tribes and the Pilgrims. God, as a noun, was the problem.

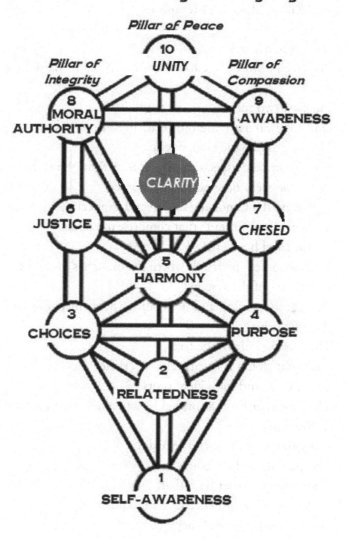

The Way of Return
Ascending
The Tree of Knowledge of Everything

Tree of Knowledge of All Things

Tree of knowledge of all things is a perfect harmonic system.

The words are attributes of God for us to learn and do and be in our lives and in our return to God. The God of your highest being. In this book, we learned the paradigm that God is a verb. Consider these traits as having or doing or being. They become the verb form.

The Tree of Knowledge as a Metaphor

Like a mighty oak
The tree of knowledge has a trunk, strong, straight, and true
The first two spheres are the trunk itself
Our self-awareness and our relatedness to others
The two solid basic components
These two core aspects are the foundation, the intrinsic values for every other aspect of the tree
The strength of knowing thyself and connecting to others is essential for all traits that comprise our souls
Balance and harmony
The section of the trunk where the branches grow is the integration of the system
Constantly moving and nourishing the connections and the nurturing
The mother lode of the tree
Each branch has a specific characteristic
The unique and individual traits
That together form a unified set of values, features, and distinctions
It began with the roots, the history
Our parents and ancestors
The influences that were there long before we were born
How our roots influence us is our choice
We live them, we feed them
We make them alive

Then we have the externals
The sunlight and the water
The elements, all the influences.
The circumstances of our lives
Then we have the intangible spirit
Unbounded and unlimited
Everlasting and enduring
Heed it or not
What is manifested
The leaves each and every season
The thoughts words and deeds
Our life itself.

Haiku

Following are haiku with seventeen syllables: first line—five; second line—seven; third line—five.

These haiku are followed by standard poems and free form on the attributes as verbs on the tree.

Personhood

self-awareness and
ego aligned to our souls
is mandatory

Inclusion Interrelate Relate

Clear contributions
Effective relationships
are the key to life

Choices

Our way of return
mastery of free-will choices
awe and gratitude

Purpose

a purposeful life
positive and filled with joy
yields blessings for all

Harmony

Harmony, balance
provide continual flow
the return to God

Justice

what and how you act
justice, justice do pursue
all aspects matter

Kindness

Kindness—a virtue
generosity and love
Unbridled goodness

Understanding

Understanding
Authority, Strength and Truth
knowledge and honor

Wisdom

Completely conscious
Inner truth, heaven and earth
Wisdom, awareness

Peace

Peace, wholeness, union
A vision for humankind
Humans being kind

Clarity

Transcendent Spirit
Illumination and light
Clarity above

The Three Pillars

Integrity

the truth, the whole truth
the full and unvarnished truth
nothing but the truth

Equilibrium

Equilibrium
Unity, fairness to all
Virtue and ethics

Compassion

Compassion, mercy
Empathy with a full heart
Never prejudice

The Infinite

Before creation
Beyond our comprehension
Limitlessness, pure

Is this your definition of God?

Poems on the Tree

Self-Awareness

This above all,
To thine own self be true
The antithesis of looking out for number one
Inner space and inner peace
Give us all the capacity
To be and let be
The goal of a well-lived life
To manifest your own best self
The you that is you
While connecting to others
As their own best selves.
As parts of a whole
Know thyself, thy whole self
Your fundamental simplicity
Without pretense and ego
The inner quietude and consistency
Always finding ways to manifest your inner truth
The core of your being,
Your essential nature and expression
Of your mind and your experience
Your reality with your soul
Your thoughts with your inner knowingness.
Your actions with your results
Once you know you at your best self
You are on the path to living your life in equilibrium
In consonance with the universe

Relatedness

It's far more than groups or charts
A title or things in a row

Interactions are the core
Helping and doing provide the flow
The basic connection is the verbs
What you do and how you feel
Attune yourself and be conscious
Appreciation seals the deal of relatedness
Be a companion and a friend
Don't ever hold back—forgive
Laugh together—be joyful
Then there's space for the hard times
Be a friend
Be family

Choices

Free-will choice, the basis for Genesis
Adam, Eve, and Noah were given
The tools and the context
To make good choices
The journey has been long and slow
Adam and Eve chose curiosity
Rather than the safety of obedience
Our lives are a continual demonstration
Of our discernment, our criteria and our values
Do we seek options
And consider a range of possibilities
Rather than react without considerations
Without contemplation or good data
The underlying, intrinsic value of this aspect
Of the tree of knowledge is integrity
Do our choices reflect our integrity
And our respect for others
We build on our choices
Day by day and year by year
We create our own patterns and standards of behavior
Our choices are the window to our egos

And conversely to our souls
Do we expand or limit choices?
Do we exploit self-vested interests?
Do we expand the options for others?
Is it dependent on your stance
Or the restriction for others
Or both?

Purpose

A positive, purposeful God
Creates our universe and all that is in it
A focus on coming and becoming
Directed and aligned
To being the best you can be
The constancy and the steadfastness
The integration of
Your body, mind and spirit
Founded and consistent with the pillar of compassion
Certainly it includes goals
To be inspired and to inspire others
Goals are essentially a target for one's personal achievements
The focus and determination
Purpose may have a more encompassing motivation
To include results for the well-being of others
Humankind and all aspects of our planet
Purpose is a calling
An aspiration that engages
Your deepest feelings
Your talents and your experiences
Into a unified whole

The Hub

Effective center for action
The fulcrum for all we do
The pivotal balance point

Connecting all that is true
Or is it our very heart·
Our core movement that leads
the nucleus of activity
Of all our thoughts acts and deeds

Justice

Justice, Justice Shalt Thou Pursue (Devarim 16:20).
It is not only what you pursue, but how you do it.
Many times, the fault is in the manner of the action.
Doing a good deed with haughtiness is the downfall.
Do good things truthfully and honorably.

Kindness

Called the Great Commandment, virtually all religions and spiritual philosophies have a version of this teaching: "You shall not take vengeance or bear a grudge against any of your people, but you shall love your neighbor as yourself: I am the Lord" (Leviticus 19:18).

Rabbi Hillel taught, "That which is hateful to you, do not do to another. That is the whole Law. The rest is commentary. Now go and learn."

Jesus, the rabbi's student at Beit Hillel, taught, "Do to others as you would have them do to you" (Luke 6:31).

Every version of this teaching is the cornerstone of this sphere. It is the embodiment of the first two spheres in action.

If it isn't nice, don't do it.

Moral Authority—The Upper Operative Sphere of the Pillar of Integrity

Set high standards
Get your facts straight
All of them
Be alert
Knowledge matters
Lead with honor and gratitude

Lead by example
Be virtuous and gracious
Be effectual and righteous
Conscientious
Always principled in all matters
Live an exemplary life
Be that which you would like others to be

Wisdom—The Upper Operative Sphere of the Pillar of Compassion

Wisdom has so many thoughts in a field of compassion, so many critical components—discernment, benevolence, awareness, empathy, humankind.

Any comment by the Dalai Lama will apply to all the concepts in a form that reflects the manifestation of enlightenment, attuned with his soul.

When listening to him, one can appreciate the upper spheres of the tree of knowledge. He is always in truth and simplicity.

"If you want others to be happy, practice compassion. If you want to be happy, practice compassion."—Dalai Lama

Peace—The Upper Operative Sphere of the Pillar of Equilibrium

Unity, universality, inspiration, insight, understanding, wholeness, balance, and harmony are possible.

Make certain our everyday lives are seen everywhere on the tree. Practice forgiveness. Laugh and join in. Togetherness matters. Experience the joy. Smiles are the universal language.

The following was Maya Angelou's expression of her life, reflective of this wholeness: "My mission in life is not merely to survive but to thrive and to do so with some passion, some compassion, some humor, and some style."

The Aha!

Moments from out of the blue
the flashes of insight
When you have groked it

THE THREE PILLARS

EQUILIBRIUM

INTEGRITY   COMPASSION

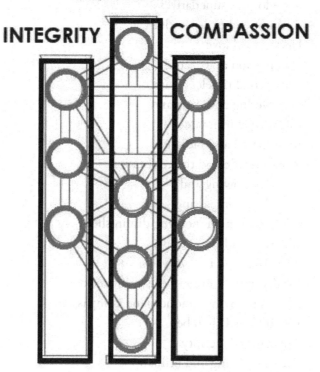

Pillar of integrity, knowledge, ethics, gratitude
Pillar of equilibrium, unity, universality, inspiration
Pillar of compassion, humankind, wisdom, benevolence

The Sphere without Limits

The connection of our souls to God
Wherein we receive in purity
And return in clarity

Pure bliss without boundaries
Our breath of life
The lightning path from God
Wherein we become human
Until our way of return
The glorious superlatives
Without end or separation
Unbounded love
Compassion at its zenith
The eternal timeless truth
Unwavering and constant
Infinite yet intimate
Illuminated and radiant
The quietude and the celebration
The all-knowing and
The all-encompassing
Nothing tainted, nothing diminished
The wise and the creative
The noble and the glory
Beauty, pure beauty in every dimension
Always in loving-kindness and compassion
I shall be as I shall be
Throughout eternity
Creating, being and brilliant
Intelligent and understanding
Pure, positive thoughts and actions
Wherein there is no place for anything
Other than love and loving
Unity, clarity and peace
Eternally

How Did the Beginning Begin?

Before creation, there was nothing. There was a void, the vast nothingness. Beyond and before existence, the act of creating began, beyond our comprehension; creating happened.

"The creation we see was made from what is not seen." The image of our Creator is not seen.

There were no nouns. Nouns must be created to exist. Creating happened before form. There had to be movement, changing. That which created is not physical, is not seen. What was created? How was action manifested? The actions, the verbs—power, will, wisdom, knowledge, understanding—aspects of intelligence far beyond our capacity

Supreme intelligence, thought, originality were the beginning.

Thinking was the first action.

The Great Disconnect

Ego

God is a verb, clear and certain action
God has no ego
Our ego is our human experience
Created in our minds
Our ego is not a verb
Our ego is not in our soul
Our ego is sourced in our mind, always
Our ego is not good or bad
It is what we make it
Our selfhood
Our point of view
Our interests, our focus
Unique and personal
Affecting all we think and do
Know who you are
Know what you do
Our problems are not created in our souls
Containing the attributes of God
Our problems are the result of how we deal with our circumstances
Our ego is a function of our choices
We create the focus of a well-lived life

Or one of self-vested interests
Even love is constricted
Unique and personal
Affecting all we think and do

EMOTU

What about the EMOTU
Ego Maniacs of the Universe
They only include that
Which affirms their ego.
For themselves, for or by others
They allow no high-quality data
They also allow no stories, no examples
Only that which supports their ego
It doesn't matter what anyone thinks
The EMOTU honor slander and perversions
Lies and distortions
Mental aberrations are our fodder
Most of all, tell us your secrets
They will teach you who hates
Get rid of your relatives
Bring your ego to us
They are dedicated to delivering the
Evil eye, the ego eye
Piercing and sinister
Intense
Given even to strangers
And the seekers
If you aren't one of us
You are against us
They include only those who support
Their egos and the absence of soul
Nothing soft, no inner knowing
Dedicated, unwavering
Nothing they cannot manipulate

They have only their ego, their mind
No traits of their souls are included
No balance, no harmony, no peace

I. Am. Ego

God has no ego, but I do
Learn to be an amigo

```
Change ego
   to
 AMIGO
```

REFERENCES

Adlerstein |, R. (n.d.). Parshas Shemos - The Source of All Freedom •
   Torah.org. Retrieved August 19, 2020, from https://torah.org/
   torah-portion/ravhirsch-5770-shemos/

Elias, A. (2020, July 17). The ten Commandments in Islam. Retrieved
   September 13, 2021, from https://www.abuaminaelias.com/
   ten-commandments-in-islam/

Goldberg, J., Ph.D. (2011, October 26). Psychoanalysis: A treatment of
   the soul. Retrieved September 03, 2021, from http://www.huffpost.
   com/entry/psychoanalysis-freud-history_b_904139

Parsons, J. (n.d.). The Hebrew names for God - El. Retrieved June 15, 2021,
   from https://hebrew4christians.com/Names_of_G-d/El/el.html

Reifler, S. (1991). *I ching: A new interpretation for modern times.* New York,
   New York: Bantam Books.

Safire, W. (n.d.). Aha! Retrieved September 06, 2021, from https://
   backissues.com/issue/New-York-Times-Magazine-February-16-1997

Selah. (2020, August 01). Retrieved August 19, 2020, from https://
   en.wikipedia.org/wiki/Selah

Tornielli, A. (2019, February 04). Pope and the Grand Imam: Historic
   declaration of peace, freedom, women's rights. Retrieved September
   28, 2020, from https://www.vaticannews.va/en/pope/news/2019-02/
   pope-francis-uae-grand-imam-declaration-of-peace.html

The Word "Selah": Ask the Rabbi Response. (n.d.). Retrieved August 19,
   2020, from https://www.aish.com/atr/The_Word_Selah.html

REFERENCES

[illegible faded reference text]

Printed in the United States
by Baker & Taylor Publisher Services